What Am I

A light-hearted search by a middle-aged insomniac to answer the questions that have always plagued him: What am I? What is consciousness? Do I really have to die?

Whilst being an autobiography of sorts, the book also deals with questions of love, science, history, nature, the media, philosophy and metaphysics.

Or, as I was hassled for a description by a smart –alec friend recently…..

It's about quantum physics, religion, history, the birth of my daughter, and the inadvisability of too many fig rolls before bedtime.

Dedicated to my pride and joy
my daughter Sonia

- JB

Index

Chapter 1: Introduction - What Am I ?

Stand and fight we do consider,
reminded of an inner pact between us
that's seen as we go.
- Jon Anderson, Gates of Delirium

Shouldn't the question be: Who am I ?

Well, I don't think so...   ...because, actually, I know *exactly* who I am.

I am a son.
I am a father.
I've been a husband.
I've been divorced.
I've been a worker.
I've been a boss.
I've been a complete prat.
I've been incredibly clever.

Yeah, yeah, yeah. Just substitute your own list. Because these are the things that make us *who* we are – well, certainly in relation to other people.

But what I mean is: lying here in the dark at 3 a.m., staring at the ceiling.
What am I ?

Well, this is always the time of night, isn't it?
When you can't sleep; these are the thoughts you have.

They say the worst time is between 2 a.m. and 6 a.m., which is why enemies always attack before the morning light, when you're at your weakest and most insecure. And sometimes, even when you're on your own, it feels the same way.
Most of the time we simply distract ourselves when such thoughts creep into our heads; we get stoned or get drunk, or work twice as hard and say, "It's all for the family."
Yep, I've done all of that for a long time – and got away with it… 'I' hardly noticed.

But it's not working tonight.

So what's the big scary problem?
Come on - I'm a mature, civilised, educated human being.
Been to hell and back. Been to heaven and back.
Seen many things. Done lots of them. Even invented some of them.

Ok, ok, ok. Let's define the question a little more simply.
Lying here, right now, at 3 a.m. in the dark, what am I ?

Yes, got it! What I mean is: right here, right now, what is this thing I call 'me'?
You know, the thing that we all consider to be about two inches behind our eyes – the bit doing the thinking! Yeah, the consciousness. The 'me'!
That's it! Well… what is it?

Of course, now that I've lived for a few decades I've begun to take 'the thinking thing inside me' so much for granted that I imagine it to be like that drunk, unruly uncle that always gets invited to the wedding – if I can get through the day without it embarrassing me then it's been a good day. And most of the time all that involves is keeping a careful watch on the brain-to-mouth connection.

Plus the fact that, on the whole, it works like my car engine – you turn the key, and it does its job. Gets me from A to B, brings home the bacon, and if necessary helps out a member of the family.

Well, that's the priorities taken care of. Time to fill up the corners with the distraction of your choice, be it television, music, chatting…

But right here, right now, none of that matters.
Because for a while, I am just me. Alone.
No use for 'the thinking thing' at the moment.
For now, it's just the 'me' behind my eyes.
Wondering what it is.

*

I suppose that part of the problem is that 'the rest of it all', 'out there', 'everything else other than me' is, well... quantifiable. You know, the pavements, the furniture, even space and galaxies, it's all 3D... isn't it.

It's all measurable. Handle-able. Solid. Almost reliable and predictable. But the fact is, that there's nothing quite like the human mind.

Let's face it, you can see that most of the universe is quantifiable, you can handle it, deal with it. But not the mind.

It's so mind-bogglingly different to everything else 'out there' as to make you think that somehow it doesn't quite fit into the big picture.

The universe goes tick-tock, clink-clank, bang-crash; and the mind seems to work like some kind of amorphous ghost – going against all the rules!

I have to admit that I love the stock answers given by the shamans and witch-doctors of our tribe (who will have their own section, later): 'three pounds of flesh', 'synaptic connections'. 'self-replicating DNA' – you have to love 'em, don't you. They don't know what consciousness actually is, but half of them would rather that you didn't realise that they don't know – else they might be out of a job.

Just take a moment... close your eyes, and consider the 'me' behind your eyes that's thinking about the 'me' behind your eyes... then open your eyes again, and look at the world.

Go on. Try it...

Close your eyes.

Think about the 'me' behind the eyes.

Then open your eyes again.

Do you see what I'm getting at? When you consider 'the mind' against the backdrop of 'the universe'... you can't help but ask, "What the hell is that!"

None of this would be so bad, except that I've got quite used to it. Being alive, I mean. Being a living being. I like it, thank-you very much, I'm enjoying being alive – there, I've said it.

*

But… oh, no! I knew 'it' was just hiding, waiting for me to open the door. The 'Other Problem'.

La-la-la-la-la! Make a lot of mental noise! Sing really annoying songs! No… it's not going to go away this time.

Because, of course, the 'Other Problem' is this: just when I got old enough to realise what being alive was all about, I then found out that one day it's all going to end. *I'm* going to end. Whether I like it or not! Now, is that the saddest joke you ever heard? – Just when I was getting the hang of it!

So the 'What am I?' question, that I was rapidly approaching being able to leave (ha-ha!) to the academics and scientists, has just had another aspect added… and this time it's serious. Now it's got personal!

*

So it's still in the third hour before dawn. I've given up trying to sleep. In fact I've made a fresh cup of tea and brought the fig-rolls upstairs, and the bedside light is on. That's how serious it is – the bedside light is on - the ultimate in self-admittance to 'thinking'. And yes (don't tell me mum!), I've just lit another cigarette.

So how did I get here? I mean, how did I 'mentally' get here.

Where did I go wrong? No-one else is awake right now pondering these things.

At least, if you ask at work tomorrow, they'll look at you like you're daft. And say "Yeah, well… did you see 'Corrie' or 'the match' on the telly last night?"

Am I cursed?

How to deal with this… how to deal with this…I know!

I can do what I've always done in the past – blame someone else!

But damn! I just remembered! This is actually *my* fault.

Damn my own mind for its memories.

I'm 20 years old, living in a bed-sit, a single room with a single bed, sink, cooker, and a chest of drawers (no wardrobe). There's a rusty old balcony where if I carefully position my single chair I can lean back and put my feet on the balcony rail. It's great for listening to the birds and the local reggae bands practising, and watching the police cars bounce into the potholes down below.

I've got clean now (-only grass eventually, but it's amazing how many hours a day *that* frees up!). I've been reading Heinlein, Krishnamurti, Buddhist philosophy, oh yeah, and how to make Pythagorean solids out of plastic toothpicks and Airfix glue. Not because I understand Pythagoras, but because they always start good conversations which end up on topics such as, "If I'm really God, then you're just a figment of my imagination that I invented to keep myself amused." (-Lawrence) and, "Of course by next year we'll have discovered the final smallest particle." (-Tony)

And somehow, somehow... I've got myself to a point where I feel free, really free. What I mean is, I owe nobody anything. Everybody around me is so busy getting involved with things, careers, love-lives – they're all too busy 'investing' themselves to be bothered with me.

Of course, I could invest in my mum's Catholic Faith... but it feels like the interest charges are too high.

I could invest in a career... but that feels like being bled slowly – touch your forelock, yes sir, no sir.

I could follow my sister... but no, I think she's had more religions than Cat Stevens.

So just plug that guitar in and start working on those scales, boyo. E flat's a pig of a key for lead guitar.

Actually, I *like* working in the music shop and playing very loud guitar in a band. Think of the future? Planning? Responsibilities? Sorry, what was that you said? I think the Marshall PA at the last gig caused some damage– my hearing keeps fading in and out.

And the only thing that's really piqued my interest otherwise, is that Krishnamurti and those Buddhist guys say that you can do it all yourself. That you don't *have* to follow anyone. You don't have to align yourself with a movement or a leader or a guru. You *can* think your own thoughts, and even, they suggest, work it all out – by yourself. For some reason, I like the sound of that.

So then I do it. Penniless, but happy, in a 10 foot by 10 foot bed-sit, I offer up:

"Dear universe, I would like to walk my own path, find my own discoveries, work out my own solutions, uncover my own answers. And yes, in return, I promise that I won't whinge or cry if I don't like what I find – so long as it's the truth."

Wow – that's like making a deal with the Devil! Except that in this case, the Devil is *me*, and cheating in a game of chess won't let me off – because *I'd* still know.

*

I'd forgotten I did that – but it's brought me all the way to here-and-now, three decades later, sitting up in bed eating fig-rolls and watching the faint light of dawn.

Putting the pieces together.

It's been a long journey, and if I have any intelligence at all then I should realise that it's not over yet; there's always room for more information, more clarification.

But for now, I have an amazing sense of peace – that the pieces really are coming together. And now it all seems so obvious.

And so, (in that time-honoured tradition) dear reader, can I show you the path I walked, and the things I found?

Oh yes, in case you're wondering, this is not *all* about me.

Hey, if I was pushing the line of 'come to me, I have all the answers' then how could I look at myself in the shaving mirror tomorrow? People who do that make me sick – 'You're lower, I'm higher', 'I'm further along the path than you are. I'll show you the way.' Stratification (with you at the bottom) - that's all *that* is.

By all means, throw your own views and opinions this way – after all, we're trying to put the big picture together, and all are welcome to contribute. I've had *no* flash of revelation – I've simply gathered together information from other people – as Newton so eloquently put it: "If I have seen a little further it is by standing on the shoulders of giants." But what a view! I think you'll like what I've found. I honestly do.

Or, perhaps some of what I've found may simply fill in some of those awkward gaps in your *own* big picture. And after all, do you know of anything more important? Especially as *you* lie there at 3 a.m. staring into the darkness.

And for those who've known me a long time, and are wondering... no, I've not 'found God' or 'got religion' – I'm still as much an atheist as I ever was...

...but (and I can't resist this, showman that I am!)...

It's all so beautiful.

Chapter 2: The Melting Pot

One of the things I've noticed over the years is that if you can't find an easily accessible answer to a problem, then very often the next best strategy is to keep throwing further questions into the melting pot. This applies not only to technical problems, but also to such vagaries as business and human relationships. Very often, at the very least, the extra questions help to redefine or clarify the original question, to the point where the extra questions begin to look like pieces of a mosaic, and a shape begins to take form.

I have to admit that if the final 'answer to life, the universe and everything' was handed to me tomorrow a few seconds before I died, I'd still have time to say, "But hey, there were a few other questions I'd have liked answered!"

So let's just line up a few of the *other* questions, and throw them into the melting pot. Perhaps just by acknowledging and including them, it will give us a pointer towards some more information, or a way of thinking, that will help with the big picture.

So these, for me, are the unanswered questions that spring immediately to mind: -

Love
What is love, actually?
Why does it feel so good?
Why does it hurt so much?
Why is a good percentage of human artistic endeavour concerned with it, if it's only about hormones?

Anomalies
These are the oddities that the shamans try to distract us from noticing. There are so many. Here are just two:-
Pi… You know, the descriptive rule of a circle. You must have noticed that Pi is involved in so many things; from the shape of the object you're standing on (the Earth), to its trajectory around the Sun, to its trajectory around the Milky Way.

Don't worry – I'm not going to get all mathematical on you – I'd only give myself a headache; but puhlease…. let's be honest: 3.142….. What the hell kind of a number is that for one of the fundamental rules of the Universe?!

The Golden Ratio: 1:1.618… Ditto, as above. This rule also appears to be fundamental, and a significant part of the tick-tock universe. And once again, what kind of a number is that, to be running things on?

Infinity

Infinity's brilliant, isn't it? You only have to go out on a star-filled night and look up.

When I was very small my mum used to tell me that when I died and went to Heaven (-naturally), it would last forever. So, of course, I tried to imagine 'forever', and ended up hanging onto the bedroom carpet with my fingernails.

And yet, there does appear to be a 'forever' or 'infinity' right here. Just look straight up. But take a deep breath first. Our witch-doctors are very offhand about it: "Oh yeah, we know all about that – we're drawing up the equations right now." (- and have been for 5,000 years.)

Well, I've yet to see any explanations that make any real human sense – just mathematical conundrums that prove mathematicians to be the incorrigible game players that we've always known them to be.

And that's the point for me – I want some *real* human answers.

I don't want religious dogma.
("Believe what I believe, and I promise that you will live forever.")

I don't want mathematical gymnastics that I can't possibly understand.
(Example? – Well, most maths theorems!)

I don't want philosophical vagaries.
("The truth is in the centre of the lotus flower.")

What I would like, if it's possible, is a real rational basis for what I actually feel. For example, it's all very well if you say, "I feel as if I'm a small part of a totally connected homogenous universe" – but is there actually any rational basis or proof for that feeling?

Still, for now, let's content ourselves with throwing in these other questions, and maybe by doing that we can sneak up obliquely on the big ones.

In the next few chapters I may appear to be introducing completely unrelated subjects, such as those mentioned above, with no possible connection between any of them.

I'd like you to trust me for now, and walk the path with me.

I assure you that it is my intention to draw them all together at the end. And, of course, throughout all of this, I will not have lost sight of the original questions: 'What Am I?' and 'Do I have to end?'

Chapter 3: Why Is Love So Important?

Broken Love – Why Does Love Hurt So Much?

How can this be love if it makes us cry?
- Andrew Gold

So I'm sitting there on my second-hand sofa, in my little two-up, two-down terraced house. Musing – as is my want. Staring into space. I had it all – the detached house and garage, the car, the wife and daughter.

It's been a three-year fight, and cost me every penny I have, just to stand still. And as is the way of the western world, the male has been skinned to the bone, though I don't honestly think the female is any better off.

And I realise – I miss her.

The woman I've known and loved, then learned to hate, at least well enough to fight both her and the authorities to a standstill – for my reputation, for my daughter, for my self-respect, for all I've worked for.

It's been three years since she walked out. 15 months of that spent looking after little Sonia, hoping she won't ask where her mother's gone, until she misses her mother so much she goes to join her. It's been an odyssey, and unbeknownst to me there's still a couple of years to go...

But enough time has passed now that I'm able to calmly examine the descent into marital hell from all angles – and even begun to see it from her point of view.

There's no going back; and I know *she* wouldn't want to. - But I miss her.

When those treacherous memories jump out, when those wistful (ahem) images catch me just as I'm falling asleep, a knife of ice in the solar-plexus...

Damn her – that smile!

There are no expletives enough to fill this page to describe how betrayed I feel...   – by myself !

Because the fact is, and I can't deny it any more, a 'connection' was made between us. In meeting, learning, growing to know each other, learning to love, having a child... a connection grew between us – an almost tangible, physical thread which became thicker and stronger the more our minds and lives were co-enjoined.

A connection which is now incredibly stretched. But still not quite broken.

*

Could it be that there actually *is* a connection, a thread, which physically/mentally ties us, still? Sometimes, against all other logic, it's the only explanation that makes any sense; and of course this allows me to be a little gentler with myself, and not scold myself too much for still feeling.

Hmmm. To be mused on.

*

Why Is Love So Rewarding?

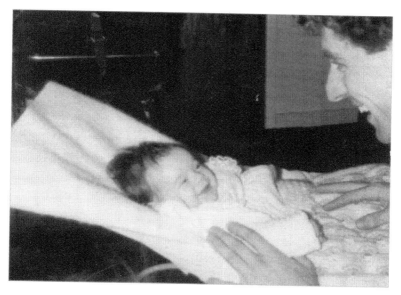

For small creatures such as we the vastness is bearable only through love.
- Carl Sagan.

14 hours of labour – many of those without a cigarette. I'd been out on the hospital balcony to watch the dawn, and was brainless with tiredness. My wife didn't seem very comfortable either. Finally the time was upon us, and even in my stupor I realised that there was no turning back now. For most of our lives, when any event happens there's always an option; even when you're sitting in a dentist's chair you can decide to leap up and run out of the door. But what was about to happen, there was no stopping; I could feel that gut-numbing coldness that told me, that apart from our own births and deaths, what was about to happen would change our lives as no other event had ever done before, or ever would again.

They had me sit on the bed behind my wife, cradling her in my arms as she delivered the baby, but I could see well enough over her shoulder.

The tiny blood-soaked creature that we'd waited so long for finally entered the world, slowly and unmoving - with the purple-grey umbilical cord wrapped around its neck. A midwife, three student nurses and myself, all stared in utter disbelief. Time froze, and all I could think was – to have carried for so long, to have gone through all that pain – all for nothing?

A young Asian doctor stuck his head around the door, took in the scene at a glance, strode over and helped the midwife cut the cord, scooped up the baby and carried her to a side table.

"5cc's of… 10cc's of…" he called out. I don't remember very well, but I think an oxygen mask was involved.

"What's happening?" groaned my wife, still riding the waves of pain despite the gas.

"It's ok, love. They're just cleaning up the baby."

The longest minute of my life.

The doctor waved me over. I gently settled my wife down onto the bed, and walked towards him. He smiled and looked down, my gaze followed his – the baby's chest was gently rising and falling. I stared in disbelief, then he picked up the baby and handed her to me. I nestled her in my arms. He smiled, and darted out of the room – I never knew his name – off to make sure that other people's worlds would not come crashing down.

I looked down, and at that moment she opened her eyes.

Deep brown almost black eyes staring straight up at me.

"Hello, little one. Welcome to the world," I whispered.

My chest was tight. I could hardly breathe.

And in my mind, "I will protect you all my life."

Then the feeling came up from my chest into my throat, and I choked.

You see, Mother Nature had pulled a fast one on me, as I suspect she does with many men. For this particular father, all through the pregnancy the baby was not a real person, but just a condition that my wife was in. I honestly couldn't feel that there was a third person involved.

At the moment the baby was put into my arms Mother Nature flicked a switch in my head that I didn't even know was there, and I was never the same again.

I can't say that I was a good father – not one of those saintly types we've all seen who change the nappies more often than the mother does. I was far too work-obsessed, following in my father's footsteps (or at least what I perceived a father should be), and eventually of course the divorce took a terrible toll on us all.

Sonia phoned today. 21 years old, a couple of months ago.

"Hey, dad, where are you?"
"Shopping, love. How are you?"
"Fine. I'm coming over on Saturday, ok?"
"Sure, but my car's off the road – in the garage."
"No problem – I'll get the bus."
"Can't give you a lift home…"
"No probs. I'll get a timetable. See you Saturday."

I need nothing from my daughter.
Nor she from me.
But just to know that each other exist in the world.
And to get together occasionally and compare notes.

The connection was made… and will go on until we die.

*

Love And Reproduction

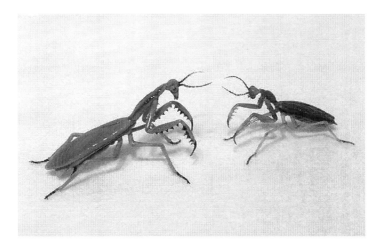

"'Ullo, mate. Gettin' any?" is usually the opening gambit from my pal Andy.

To which I usually reply, "As you know full well, Andrew, my own sensitivities lie in a more spiritual direction which takes into account the refined, esoteric and emotional needs of the opposite gender."

"Ah… The answer's 'no' then."

I'm still trying to work out whether Andy seriously believes what he expresses as a maxim: that love is a biological fantasy; it's only purpose to aid reproduction.
(Andy was also a single male parent to his two children while they were growing up; but best not to remind him of that. He'll just bark at you: "So?")

In the picture above, the male praying mantis (the smaller one on the right) will cautiously circle around and approach the female from behind. In actual fact it will do him no good, because even as he is mating with her she will reach around and bite off his head, and begin to eat it. Strangely, the rest of his body will carry on as if it hasn't noticed, and the insemination will be completed. (Many female humans claim to have also experienced a not dissimilar behaviour in human males.) The female praying mantis will then eat the rest of the male praying mantis' body; after all she must keep up her strength, and think of her future children.
Strange, but true – I've seen the film that this photo came from.

Reproduction does not need love.
The praying mantis is just one of the many species that proves the point.

So what is it with love and human beings? Because obviously we don't need love in order to reproduce; though most of us would agree that it greatly aids reproduction, pair-bonding and child-nurturing.

*

Altruistic Love

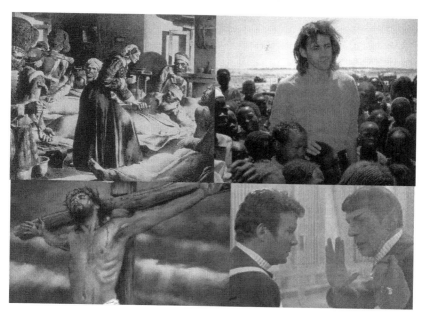

From Florence Nightingale through to Bob Geldof, take a walk through history and see many examples of altruistic love. Both were significant, in that they were wealthy people who would normally have been expected to spend their days reclining and sipping wine, but found themselves unable to continue their existence without dedicating their lives to helping others.

The 2000 year-old story of Jesus accepting his torture and death as a necessary sacrifice for others has been told and retold, and cited as a perfect example of the purest form of love.

Even modern literature and new media provide ideals of personal sacrifice: "The needs of the many outweigh the needs of the few. Or the one." – The scene of Spock's selfless death for his shipmates never fails to induce tears.

Why tears? Because tears - and the inability to breathe, and the choking feeling in the throat - are the human body and mind's way of saying, "Just in case you haven't noticed, this is *incredibly* important."

The fact is, that altruistic love is generally held by humans to be the most perfect form of love. Even Shakespeare, despite his many examinations of personal love, affection and lust, says...

> Love is not love
> Which alters when it alteration finds,
> Or bends with the remover to remove:
> O, no! it is an ever-fixed mark,
> That looks on tempests and is never shaken;
> It is the star to every wandering bark,
> Whose worth's unknown, although his height be taken.
> Love's not Time's fool, though rosy lips and cheeks
> within his bending sickle's compass come;
> Love alters not with his brief hours and weeks,
> But bears it out even to the edge of doom.
> If this be error, and upon me prov'd,
> I never writ, nor no man ever lov'd.
> - Shakespeare - Sonnet 116

...and makes it very clear that he is describing a more general, pure form of love, from which all other forms of love spring.

The fact is, that love manifests itself in the world in many forms, from physical attraction all the way through to total altruism and self-sacrifice.

Love creates life, cherishes life, preserves life.

I *would* dispute that there could be such a thing as 'selfish love' (at the other end of the scale from altruistic love?), since with even a little experience of being alive one soon comes to realise that the two words *selfish* and *love* are mutually incompatible in meaning.

The problem is, that it actually begins to look as if there is a thing called 'love'. A force, an idea, an energy, that manifests itself into many different forms depending on the circumstances. Ah... what a romantic idea.

But could it be true?

Chapter 4: Learning and Education – what's the point?

"Why bother to learn? Why bother to explore? - Everything's already known."

Whoso neglects learning in his youth, loses the past and is dead for the future.
- Euripides

I not only use all the brains that I have, but all that I can borrow.
- Woodrow Wilson

Learning

Sonia's friends sometimes allow me (- an old man, as they see me) to sit with them while they're chatting. I think some of them are actually intrigued to see if there is any similarity between my view and their views, despite the three-decade age gap.

One of them had asked me what I was 'into these days', and I had replied that I was reading up on multiple dimensions, even though I had no formal training in physics (hah-hah, and I'm sure I still sound very clever).

One of their reactions absolutely stopped me dead.

A young man, Craig, sitting cross-legged with his hair falling over his face, had mumbled, "What's the point?"

"Pardon?" I said (-I'm quick like that).

"Well, what's the point? Why bother? Everything's already known."

"Duh?" (-erudite, as ever.)

"Yeah. It's all on the telly, on the science programs. Or you just search the Internet."

"Such as what?"

"Well, you know, black holes, the big bang, the speed of light. It's all known. Just do a search."

And of course, the rest of them just nodded.

Well, I don't know what kind of schooling *you* had, but mine was a strange mixture of absolute Catholic dogma contrasted with an overall philosophy of: 'All you have to do is get out there, discover new things, and make it all happen.' Admittedly, this *was* decades ago, but had things changed *so* much in the meantime? I mean, I grew up in an era that had followed hard on the heels of the invention of the atom bomb, the first computer, revolutions in chemistry, physics, biology, the discovery of DNA, and finally the first steps on the moon. The unspoken feeling behind *my* education was simply this: 'Just get out there, overthrow current theories, create new ones, there's always room for advancement and changes – and well, in fact, we expect you to.'

So I phoned my friend Liz, a teacher, spluttering "And then I mentioned Priestley and Einstein, and the mistakes they made…"

"John, they've probably never heard of Einstein."

"Of course they've heard of Einstein. Everybody's heard of Einstein."

"They have - if they've been taught history and science. Otherwise he's just the silly bloke with the fluffy hair."

"Sorry, Liz, you lost me there. How could they *not* be taught history?"

"Because, generally it's not taught in schools anymore."

"What are you talking about? It's the basis. It's the framework… I mean, I hated it, but it's the backdrop to all other subjects!"

"The present government has declared history to be one of the 'wooley' subjects, along with philosophy and a few others, and so it is now *not* one of the mandatory subjects."

"Liz — are you telling me that there's no history being taught in schools at all?"

"Well, history is now considered to be part of the social sciences. And is taught by the Social Science teacher. Or not."

"And if the Social Science teacher doesn't know any history..."

"It doesn't get taught."

Perhaps I have an overly suspicious nature, but if you wanted to create a 'new era', politically speaking, and ideally you would prefer people *not* to ask what alternatives there might be to your political party — in fact not even raise the question of an alternative — then the best ploy would be to remove the memories of any previous political systems from their minds; or even better, make sure they didn't learn about those previous political systems in the first place.

So why do images of Stalin's efforts to rewrite Russian history, and the Nazi book-bonfires, spring to mind? Come home, George Orwell. All is forgiven.

So these kids feel that there's no point exploring, questioning, learning. It's all been done, it's all known, it's all 'locked down'. And consequently it's all pointless.

So who's telling them this? And is it, in fact, true?
But hang on — this is not just about the kids, either.

After all, we hear every other day that '50 is the new 40'.

In other words, people are living longer and more healthily, and it's now a common occurrence that what we used to call 'middle-aged people' are *not* prepared to conveniently roll over and die, but still have one or two functioning brain cells and are determined to use them.

If we wish to answer important questions (like those we started with) we need *sound* information, and of course we're not just talking about which horse won the race, or how the stock market closed.

We *are* being given sound information, aren't we, by our shamans?

Perhaps we'd better check this out.

After all, when you're asking 'What's my place in the universe?' you first need good information *about* the universe.

Well… why not - let's use the three topics that Craig mentioned, as a test.

*

The speed of light - 186,000 miles per second – it's the law!

It is [the] belief in absolutes, I would hazard,
that is the great enemy today of the life of the mind.
- Arthur Schlesinger Jr.

We all know this. We were taught it in school.

And of course the speed of light, we are told, is a constant.

Absolute. Inviolable. Unchanging.

Well, thank goodness for that! At last - something 'solid' we can hang on to. And of course, thank goodness again – the physicists have an absolute, unchanging unit on which to base all their other calculations. Even a casual search will bring up typical definitions: 299,792,458 metres per second, 300 million metres per second, 186 thousand miles per second (the one I learned at school). A typical quote is: "The speed of light, sometimes known as "C" (as in E=MC^2), is a constant of the Universe." [2]

Every science program on the television which mentions it tells us that the speed of light is a constant, *really* a constant; and that nothing, absolutely nothing, can go faster than the speed of light; not even the Enterprise. Ever.

If I remember rightly, heavier-than-air flight was impossible, and 'everyone knew this'. Not to mention the fact that the first steam locomotives were criticised for their excessive speed, since everyone 'knew' that if you went faster than 30 miles an hour you'd burn up due to air friction.

The world is moving so fast these days that the man who says it can't be done is generally interrupted by someone doing it.
- Harry Emerson Fosdick

Given the contrary nature of humankind, especially when faced with supposed absolutes, I shouldn't be surprised that researchers at Princeton say that the speed of light *can* be pushed beyond known boundaries, at least under laboratory conditions. And Lijun Wang, a researcher with the private NEC Institute says, "However, our experiment does show that the generally held misconception that 'nothing can travel faster than the speed of light' is wrong." [3] [4]

But hang on - I've watched plenty of science programs since that report in July 2000, and none of them have mentioned this!

In fact, in the few months between beginning this research, and writing this chapter, more and more Internet references show articles describing experiments which concur with that first one – one even describing how two student physicists have created a piece of equipment (for $500!) through which they have accelerated the speed of light by a factor of 4! [5]

In turn, the scientific web pages are now using phrases such as "The speed of light is constant only in the absolute space-time frame, ... The question whether the speed of light is a true physical limit has no definite..."

So obviously, the scientific community (our shamans) are coming clean with us as they make their discoveries.

So why aren't the media?

The Big Bang

I'm still looking for 'fundamental information', and how much more fundamental can you get, than the Big Bang?

Ah, yes. I remember this one.

And the key hypothesis was, of course, 'from a uniform point'.

Shall we all say that together: 'From - A - Uniform - Point.' (Thank-you.)

Hmm - I have a slight problem −

The results of the Big Bang

NASA photo from the Hubble Space Telescope
– equivalent to a 1-inch section in a 6-foot diameter sphere.

- Does this look uniform to you?

I'm obviously misunderstanding something, here. So let's go back to *when* the Big Bang was discovered, shall we? I mean – I am all right using the word 'discovered', aren't I?

If a respected science writer such as Simon Singh who writes for the BBC ("Fermat's Last Theorem") can call his new book – 'The Big Bang: The Most Important Scientific Discovery of All Time and Why You Need to Know About It' - then it's obviously a discovery, with facts. Isn't it?

But when we go to the 'horse's mouth', NASA, they say that the Big Bang Theory is the 'dominant' scientific theory about the origin of the universe:

The big bang was initially suggested because it explains why distant galaxies are travelling away from us at great speeds... Although the Big Bang Theory is widely accepted, it probably will never be proved; consequentially, leaving a number of tough, unanswered questions.
- NASA 1997 [6]

So the scientific community are once again being honest, and calling it either a 'dominant scientific theory', or very often a 'premise'; but the media are generally selling the information to us using the labels 'discovered' and 'proved'.

Are we seeing a pattern here?

*

Black Holes

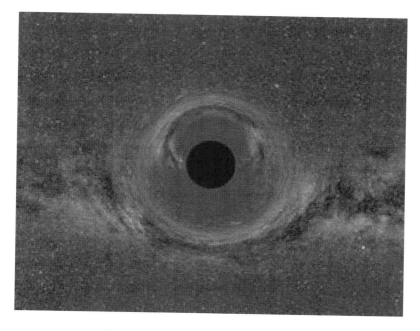

I have done a lot of work on black holes,
and it would all be wasted if it turned out
that black holes do not exist.
- Stephen Hawking, A Brief History of Time

Woo – scary. The cosmic equivalent of Delhi-belly. There ain't no resistance to *this* mother.

It must be 30 years since I read my first book on Black Holes (and of course didn't understand a word of it), so surely by now there must be a ton of real evidence (and I *do* mean real), and some hard facts.

Stuart Robbins (Case Western Reserve University, Ohio, majoring in Astronomy and double minoring in Physics and Geology) says, "No black hole has actually been imaged in a telescope." [7]

Hang on Stuart, you may be just one of the small fish – let's see what the big boys have to say.

NASA says:

There are many popular myths concerning black holes, many of them perpetuated by Hollywood... It can be said that black holes are really just the evolutionary end point of massive stars. But somehow, this simple explanation makes them no easier to understand or less mysterious. [8]

New Scientist says:

After nearly 30 years of arguing that a black hole destroys everything that falls into it, Stephen Hawking is saying he was wrong. Though Hawking has not yet revealed the detailed maths behind his finding.[9]

Woah. Sorry... I'm just the interested observer around here. Can I make sure I understand this?
- The picture above is a 'made-up' picture?
- No black hole has actually been imaged in a telescope?
- Black Holes have been theorised in physics via mathematics, but never actually seen or proven?
- Even now, Stephen Hawking is contradicting himself on what he does, or does not, 'know'?
- Hawking himself says: "I have done a lot of work on black holes, and it would all be wasted if it turned out that black holes do not exist." -? [10]

I have to admit that a black hole (as described in the literature) is the only thing that would make sense, at the centre of the Galaxy; and maybe under other circumstances.

Once again, the scientific community appear to be being honest (well... eventually), but what I object to is that I'm again being 'sold' Black Hole *theories* as fact. Hey, I *have* the T-shirt!

Education

"Because I say so!" yelled the teacher, spinning around and hurling the wooden board-duster at the boy at the back of the class.

I was *not* that boy. I'd already learned to stay quiet. 100% of the time.
I'd also learned that we all existed in a strange reality where saying, "Excuse me, sir, I didn't quite follow that. Could

you go over it again?" had absolutely no effect on the maths teacher, who just continued to write on the board.

Marching to his own drum, obviously.

The question that had prompted the outburst was, "Sir, this calculus – why do we have to learn it?"

It would have been so nice if he'd said, "Well – you know the rockets that are going up, and the proposed moon-landing next year? All the calculations that ensure that the astronauts get to the moon and cleanly orbit it, instead of smashing into it, are all done by calculus."

I can guarantee that he would have had a classroom of boys leaping up and down, wanting to know more.

But this never happened. In any subject.

"Sir, what do you think of the new satellite photos showing the curvature of the Earth?" We should have known better - this was aimed at the religion teacher, after all.

"They're all faked. The bible says the Earth is flat. By the way, I'm a member of the Flat Earth Society."

I assure you that it *is* possible for a classroom of boys to remain motionless, eyes wide, eyebrows raised, and know exactly what each other are thinking.

Possible. But it takes practice. We had lots of that.

Dear Mr Heslop (the only lay teacher in the school), you tried so hard with your humour and your humanity, and I was doing fine through the Romans, and the Normans, and even the Tudors, but I finally fell asleep around the 'corn laws' and the 'window tax'. Much, much, later I realised: *What* a backdrop you had given me for all my other learning. A sense of time, of change, of context.

But overall, that was the problem – we were never taught 'the reason why'. In any subject.

After the ability to band together as a team, the greatest strength of the monkey that came down from the trees is the ability to pass on our learning. And of course an integral part of that knowledge is 'the reason why'.

Now, if the essence of what we teach is that 'it's all known', then we may as well give up and go home. And of course that's exactly what history *does* teach us: it's *never* all known. Scary - but exciting.

Maybe it's time we took a closer look at scientists. These are, after all, the aforesaid 'shamans of the tribe' who we, as a society for the last 5000 years, have paid to do our thinking and investigating for us. Let's face it, the rest of us are too busy digging ditches and having babies.

But can we trust them?

Chapter 5: Scientists, Superstars and Shamans

And they're the same species as us, are they?

I've always had the greatest respect for scientists – they are so damn clever aren't they? Ideas that they routinely juggle with, even before breakfast, I could not begin to understand.

I have to admit that whenever I start to read definitions and formulae such as the speed of light in the last section, after the first line my mind just goes skipping out to play. La-la-la-la-la. No, don't make me read those theorems – I know I'll just get a headache.

I *have* had the good fortune to know and work with some of them.
And I can tell you – they're human.
Just.
You *could* invite them home for dinner – no problem. But by the end, you'd be wondering - exactly *which* bit has been lobotomised?

As a society, we have no conscience about using these lovely people to our own ends. In fact we *pay* them to have flights of fancy – hey, otherwise we'd still be living in mud huts. Either directly or indirectly, they are responsible for the roof over my head, the car I drive, the computer I'm typing this on, and certainly the life of my daughter.
On the whole, I come away with the impression that they are only too eager to be of service, to better humanity; so long as their massive egos are given enough acclaim, they're simple folk with an almost guileless attitude to life. And if they occasionally get something wrong, well, it'll all come out in the wash won't it, onward and upward.

But what I'm aware of is…
if we're not to be manipulated by charlatans
("Believe what I believe, and you'll be saved.")
if we're not to be confounded by semantic gymnastics
("The answer is in the centre of the lotus.")

if we're not to be confused by the strength of our own longings, and wishful natures

("I'm sure my dad is watching over me.")

... then these clever-clogs are possibly our only hope of gathering together sober, unbiased knowledge which we can use to answer our original questions.

Why does that thought *not* fill me with confidence?

After all, we are *so* often told "When Einstein proved...", and that's all that needs to be said, surely?

Let's take a closer look at a few examples, over the years, of the people that we have to rely on for the truth of all things.

Joseph Priestley (1733-1804)

Priestley was fairly typical of his age, in that there were no professional scientists as we now know them; they called themselves 'philosophers', or 'natural philosophers', and were pretty much self-financed.

He was actually a clergyman turned chemist, who researched the relationship between plants, animals and air (that's actually quite ground-breaking, if you think about it). He isolated oxygen (1774) and discovered hydrochloric and sulphuric acid (1775).

But the reason yours truly remembered him from school was his 'Phlogiston Theory', which postulated that 'in all flammable materials there is present phlogiston, a substance without colour, odour, taste, or weight that is given off in burning.'

The Phlogiston Theory held sway, and had many loyal adherents, for over 20 years, until Antoine-Laurent Lavoisier effectively showed that combustion requires oxygen. **[11]**

In other words, effectively 100% wrong - which doesn't make him any less brilliant in his other discoveries, but just very humanly dogmatic.

Albert Einstein

Ah – good old Albert.

Saint Albert, who was never wrong. Apparently. If we believe the Media.

Except that he was. Often. At least 8 times. **[12]**

In 1917, in what he would later call "the greatest blunder of my life," Einstein added a term called 'lambda' to his equations that would make his calculations consistent with a static universe. Einstein admitted his mistake in 1929.

Let me just make sure I understand this…
- Albert's equations didn't balance,
- So he added a new value (lambda), not knowing or specifying what that value could be ("It's just zis thing, you know?"), just to make them add up.
- And later retracted it, when he was proven wrong.
…Have I got that right?

The University of Southern California are quite outspoken about this: "Einstein's theory of gravity has now been disproved (2004). Soon after it's completion [the early 1900's], the theory of quantum mechanics was developed. General Relativity seems to be incompatible with quantum mechanics and breaks down."- **[13]**

Hmm… Now I *am* confused. Like most people, I've always had the impression that the General Theory of Relativity is as solidly factual and proven as any theory can be.

The Journal of Young Investigators says:

"though it appears one of his blunders may be less of a mistake than he thought. The cosmological constant Einstein created (lambda), then later retracted, may explain the acceleration of dark energy, according to new research from the Supernova Legacy Survey (SLS)." [14]

So the 'deliberate mistake' that Albert put into his original equations (we won't call it a 'con' ;-) to justify his erroneous belief in a 'steady-state universe' actually turned out to be the missing ingredient for the 'expanding universe' theory.

Woah! High-five! How lucky is that!

One tale I love about Einstein is the fact that he never actually said that Time was the fourth dimension. Apparently a journalist, on listening to his theories replied, 'So that means that Time is the fourth dimension?' And Einstein, faced with a crowd of clamouring news-hacks at the end of a long, hard day sighed disparagingly, 'Yes, if you say so.'

Obviously, Einstein was an incredibly clever man, and many of his theories form the basis of modern physics, but he was also *very* much a human being (-you *don't* want to know about his private life).

So, having been wrong so many times, why do the Media constantly portray him as perfection personified; in fact as the next best thing to Mother Theresa?

Stephen Hawking

Ah, that poor man. As some would have us believe, the most intelligent man that has ever lived... and they put him in a Simpsons cartoon!

And you daren't criticise him – that would be like kicking a living saint!

All of this is, of course, according to the media, who say: "Hawking revolutionized the study of the holes when he demonstrated in 1976 that, under the strange rules of quantum physics, once black holes form they start to "evaporate" away, radiating energy and losing mass in the process." **[15]**

What! He demonstrated? I hope they stood well back.

Well, I've read 'A Short History of Time', and of course I couldn't make head or tail of it. But at least it's there, isn't it? Still for sale. Still quoted on television, and in newspapers and magazines. Despite my jollity, the 'facts', the 'proof' – they are there for all to read and understand.

Except that New Scientist now tells us that after nearly 30 years of arguing that a black hole destroys everything that falls into it, Stephen Hawking is now saying he may have been wrong. **[16]**

The essence of which is:

Hawking has a new theory about black holes which goes against his own previous theory. (Ok... Well, we're getting used to this.)

His original theory ran counter to the rules of quantum mechanics and is known as the black hole information paradox. (Ouch.)

The paradox was found by other scientists. (Whoops.)

Hawking then revised his theories. (Whew.)

And what does he stand to lose - other than his reputation?

An encyclopaedia - the object of the bet that he started with his friend 30 years ago. Gosh, life sure is tough for these people.

And of course Stephen himself says:

"I have done a lot of work on black holes, and it would all be wasted if it turned out that black holes do not exist." **[10]**

What, Stephen? After all that, you're not even sure they exist?

Joking aside, there is no way that I am going to stand looking over Stephen Hawking's shoulder checking his calculations. And neither are you.

This *is* the cutting edge of science, and at least Stephen's honest about the situation - eventually. But we're still looking at the problem of the acquisition of sound knowledge.

So ladies and gentlemen, I think it's time to focus our mental gun sights on the culprit so far: - The Media.

The fact is: The Media can't sell 'maybes' – so don't blame the scientists. If we're really interested, and I can't emphasise this enough, don't trust the Media – dig deeper. And that's all there is to say about it.

The Scientific Method

So, is there some overall method by which scientists deduce their information?

Yes, there is – and it's called 'The Scientific Method', and I think in the broadest sense it's been with us for as long as we've been upright. So it's actually very simple.

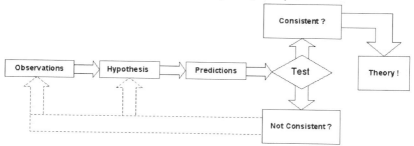

I've often heard it said: "I hate science". Well, by all means hate the scientific community if you must, but 'science' itself would be better referred to as 'the scientific method', and that's completely different.

The method is usually described like this: -

1. *Observe* some aspect of the universe.
2. Invent a tentative description; call it a *Hypothesis*.
3. Use the hypothesis to make *Predictions*.
4. *Test* those predictions by experiments or further observations.

If the tests are consistent, then we have a theory. If not, we modify the hypothesis and test again. And again.

Oh, and finally, we let everyone else test the results as well.

As a simple example…

Observation: Look at that big shiny thing in the sky.
Hypothesis: It's a huge ball of fire 3 miles wide.
Prediction: It's going to fall down and kill us all.

…the rest, you can work out.

So that's: Observation > Hypothesis > Prediction > Test.
And *don't* be afraid to reject the hypothesis if the test proves that the prediction was wrong.

And thanks to that method, we finally (after many trials and errors) get many useful things, from the computer I'm typing on, to the mobile phone, to the novacane that ensured a completely painless removal of that damn tooth-nerve the other day, and on, and on...

"Advances in medicine and agriculture have saved vastly more lives than have been lost in all the wars in history."
- Carl Sagan

"In science it often happens that scientists say, 'You know that's a really good argument; my position is mistaken,' and then they would actually change their minds and you never hear that old view from them again. They really do it. It doesn't happen as often as it should, because scientists are human and change is sometimes painful. But it happens every day. "
- Carl Sagan

So there we have it – from one of the best: admittance of human frailty, but the willingness to acknowledge mistakes, and then to try and try again.

And I don't think we can ask for more.
But I still don't have my information.

Where can I look?

Chapter 6: Anomalies – diversions or clues?

Through every rift of discovery some seeming anomaly
drops out of the darkness, and falls, as a golden link,
into the great chain of order.
- Edwin Hubble Chapin

Thank goodness for the Carl Sagans of this world who make it their personal mission to explain the complicated stuff to the rest of us.

Even so, be prepared to be very sceptical, and don't be embarrassed to ask what you feel might be considered stupid questions – after all, either directly or indirectly, we pay these people to perform this service for the rest of our tribe – and don't be afraid to be the one at the back of the class who puts her hand up and says: "Excuse me, but would you mind explaining that again?"

Unfortunately, the fact remains that if I wanted to study astronomy, or physics, or mathematics, to the point where I could read and understand even a portion of the information that scientists have already found, then each subject would take – at my guess – at least 10 years. Not to further the learning in that subject you understand, but merely to come up to speed with what has already been discovered, enough to make some sense of it.

And I simply don't have the time. The fuse is burning.

Believe me, I don't kid myself – it takes a particular type of mind to be an academic explorer – and I *don't* have that type of mind.

It reminds me of the number of people who have said to me: "I'm sure I *could* play guitar like you, if only I knew where to put my fingers."

So – where to go… where to go… Have I reached an impasse?

The only remote possibility is that there might be another route, another means of finding fundamental information, even if I only add more questions to the melting pot. And of course there has always been that scary, niggling, fact at the back of my mind: that there exist 'anomalies' that even the scientists can't explain or rationalise.

These anomalies are gaps in their understanding, unresolved phenomena of nature that get swept under the carpet or treated as inconsequential 'niggles' in the fabric of the Universe. Could it be that *they* might be more important than they first appeared?

Picture me, night after night, poor worried little creature pacing the carpet – or in *my* case, slumped on the sofa, lighting yet another cig…

But the mind is a wonderful thing, and a constant surprise even to its owner. And then the memory came back to me…

I can see the wood-grain in the old, battered table. I can smell the lager – the best in Salford – and hear the quiet laughter of the couple in the corner, and the muted sounds of the traffic outside…

Pi and a pint, please landlord.

It's 1976, and slap-bang in the middle of the progressive rock era (yay!) I'm sitting in a dingy pub in Salford on my half-day off from the music shop, nursing a half-pint and waiting for the members of 'Gentlemen' to arrive. We get together most weeks on a Thursday to ask 'How's your band doing?' and put the world to rights.

Gentlemen had the distinction of hitting, and simultaneously missing, the big-time on the very night that the Sex Pistols were first broadcast. I was there in the audience at Granada Studios to support my friends, and I remember it well.
My daughter asked me recently: "What was it like?"
I replied: "There was a stunned silence."
She said: "Well, that's to be expected."
I said: "No, you don't understand. First on were The Bowles Brothers – a 3-piece playing acoustic guitars, tight acapella harmonies, very 1940s. Not my sort of thing normally, but I loved them – bought their album eventually. Then Gentlemen blew the audience away. Let's put it this way, if all had gone well, you would never have heard of Queen. Howie *was* a better singer than Freddie Mercury. And finally the Sex Pistols. After their first number, there was complete silence. The members of the audience just looked at each other. When the Pistols started their second number half the audience got up and left as fast as they could. I stayed because like everyone

else I was waiting for the floor manager to run on and shout, 'Hah - got you! – April Fool!' "

So Gentlemen file into the pub, get their drinks, and work hard at smiling with confidence. Sure, their manager's 'making calls as we speak'. I just make sure I'm sitting next to Jimmy, their ex-guitarist, who plays finger-style electric guitar, and is in my opinion second only to Steve Howe.

"So, how's it going?" he asks.

"Going well, Jim."

"Practising?"

"5 hours a night, Jim, on average."

"Good," and he leans back, with his usual Buddha-like countenance, and sips his pint.

"Er, Jim?" This is going to be difficult. This guy's years ahead of me – I mean, he has a *Gibson* guitar - respect is an inadequate word, but I have to do this, even if it means that he will verbally demolish me with his usual quiet, pragmatic certainty of everything.

"Jim, I was working on harmonies last night."

"Yeah?"

"A slow arpeggio up the neck, then another one in harmony above it."

"Mm?"

"And then a third above that."

"And?"

"Jim, I can't explain it, but it began to look as if there were patterns in the harmonies."

"That's because there are."

"But, I mean, when you take the idea further up the neck the shapes just loop around and eventually repeat – the same patterns just keep reforming."

"Yep."

"But, I mean, it felt like there was some kind of structure, some kind of rule or plan behind it all, that I couldn't quite see…"

"And how did you feel?"

"Well, I can't explain it… I had tears in my eyes."

I don't think I'm visibly cringing – but this is my hero, after all. I wait for the onslaught.

"That's nothing," he says. "You should check out the Golden Ratio."

What! I expect a verbal tongue-lashing in response to my over-active, over-emotional imagination by one of the clearest thinkers I've ever met – and his reply is 'maths'?

Jim sits back and takes another sip, looking smug. But there again, I think he was born with that look.

"Check out the Golden Ratio," he repeats.

"And the Golden Ratio is…?"

"The ratio of one to one point six one eight."

Jim used to work in the music shop. He's the one who, when a customer accused him of being deliberately intellectual, replied, "I don't see why *I* should apologise for *your* lack of education."

He looks serene. I look vacuous. He sighs.

"Think of a nautilus sea-shell; the Golden Ratio. Think of the arrangement of petals in a sunflower; the Golden Ratio. Leaves to twigs, twigs to branches, branches to trunk. Leonardo played with the idea – you know, his sketch of the man with his arms outstretched?"

I sit back, shaking my head. "Jim – you're telling me the universe has 'rules'? A basic formula? Built in? For growth?… But what could music have to do with that? Music's man-made."

Life got busy after that. A wife, a divorce. A new wife, a baby, a new job. "Life is what happens while you're busy making plans," said John Lennon. And two and a half decades slid busily by without me noticing.

But the idea hid away. And waited.

Pi on a Welsh Hillside

The fire crackles and pops like a contented kid with a cap-gun. The meal's over, the pots are washed. We've all got our drinks, and we're all feeling very mellow, especially since we can clearly hear the wind whistling around the Welsh countryside outside, trying to get in under the door.

I've phoned my mum, and got no answer, as usual. She's out dancing. Again. At 86 years of age. My dad died 12 years ago, but Ted, the new boyfriend, has a wicked sense of humour, and has probably already added a decade to my mum's life expectancy.

I've phoned Sonia, and "My new boyfriend's a pain, but what can you do, Dad? But the job starts on Monday! When are you coming back? Give Sandy a kiss for me. Gotta run!"

Mary and Jane bought the farmhouse and the land in preparation for their retirement, which is probably never going to happen. Viv and Melissa, and Sandy and I, have come over for a winter weekend. Good company, good food, good conversation. Sandy and I are both straight – trust me on this, Sandy's straight – but Mary and Jane, and Viv and Melissa, have had decades-long relationships, longer than most straight marriages I know.

I chuckle at the thought that maybe I've become an honorary lesbian.

We've all been brave and wrapped up warm (double pants, double socks, five layers above the waist, and a woolly hat and gloves for me) and trekked across the countryside for a couple of hours, just so that the locals don't think we're city wimps. I've even washed my hands and face in the river.

I feel completely self-righteous, and I may even thaw out before it's time for bed. I lounge back and watch the shadows dance among the oak beams of the farmhouse, and for a while I'm at peace.

During a quiet moment in the conversation, Sandy leans over and whispers in my ear, "Did I mention that Melissa's a mathematician – the daughter of one of the code-breakers from Bletchley Park? You know - the Enigma Code?"

I come wide-awake. This is too good a chance to miss.

But I don't want to disgrace myself. What's the best method? I know, obeisance *always* works. That, and the willingness to admit that you actually know bugger-all about what you're asking.

I wait for a lull in the conversation, then say plaintively, "I wish I knew more about maths. I totally failed it at school."

Melissa shrugs; such a statement is obviously an admittance of being barely human. She also speaks, I think, five languages. Like a native.

I continue, "I mean…" oh dear, I sound like a 12 year old, "…what's the big deal with Pi?"

"How do you mean?" asks Melissa.

"Well, I mean. 3.142," I gesture disgustedly.

"3.1415926359…" says Melissa, eventually breaking up into a smile.

"Yeah, well. Twenty-two over seven."

"No, it's not," replies Melissa.

"What? I was taught in school that it's twenty-two divided by seven. Everyone's taught that."

"Except that it isn't," replies Melissa calmly. "That's just an approximation – an everyday, working value for Pi – good enough for making sure that beer-barrels are round, I suppose."

I'm getting *really* good at that blank look – I've had decades of practice.

"Ok… so what value of Pi would *you* use to calculate a circle?"

"Well actually, mathematically speaking – which is what I think you're asking – it's the other way round. Any idiot can draw a circle using a pin, a piece of string, and a pencil. What we're trying to do is to calculate Pi – the rule *for* that circle. In fact, the rule for any circle. In other words we start with the circle, and then try to calculate Pi."

"Which now stands at a million decimal places," chipped in Viv.

"Probably more like two million by now, love; now that they're using computers. But who's counting."

"But don't you find it fascinating?" I gasp.

"Why?"

"Because it's a non-repeating decimal that's so long that it seems to disappear into infinity; and it's such an irrational number – considering it's one of the rules of the universe!" Thankfully, nobody shoots me down over that.

"Actually, no. I don't," says Melissa.

"You don't?"

"No."

It was then that I learned a new lesson. That there *are* people who have a full, working, detailed, intimate knowledge of an incredible idea, far beyond the ken of normal man, and who still treat it as an everyday thing.

But I'm afraid I can't.

Chapter 7: Hunting the Snark

A wonderful harmony arises from joining together the seemingly unconnected.
- Heraclitus c.500 BC

Let's just remind ourselves — the mathematical value Pi is something that baffles even the egg-heads. Oh yes, they can calculate Pi to thousands of decimal places, and use it to create near-perfect circles for all sorts of functions, but they cannot explain why, as a number, it never ends.

So, I think we're going to need Melissa again to explain it. And this is the important bit: I have a feeling that it will end up in our melting pot, since we seem to have found something else, other than the human mind itself, which is (a) fundamental, and (b) an anomaly, within this universe.

Ok, Melissa, you're on. Pleeease try to explain it to the rest of us who haven't got an IQ the size of a PIN number.

Pi - what's it good for?

"Melissa... Pi - what's it good for?"

"What's it good for? Well, calculating a circumference."

(Circumference = Pi multiplied by Diameter)

"Oh yeah, I remember - the distance around the outside of a circle is equal to the diameter (the distance across the circle) multiplied by Pi. Yay – that was simple. What else?"

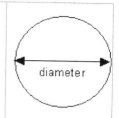

"Calculating the area contained within a circle."

(Area = Pi times Radius times Radius)

"I remember that one – the old πr^2 formula! Any more?"

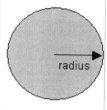

"Calculating the volume of a sphere."

(Volume = 4/3 times Pi times Radius times Radius times Radius)

"Got it. $4/3*\pi r^3$ it's usually written. Can't think why I'd need to know that though."

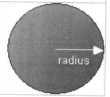

"Pi can also be used to calculate all sorts of things, like the cross sections of cylinders and cones. [19] Which is exactly the sort of calculation you need to orbit a rocket around the moon. John, do stop yawning."

"Yawning? Me? Well ok, I was. I mean, it's just a thingy, a sort of tool, isn't it, invented by people to do a job?"

"On the contrary, circles existed everywhere even before life came along. We didn't invent them – the universe is full of them – from the shape of the planet you're standing on, to the orbit it takes around its star, to the orbit that takes around it's galaxy. What people have actually been doing is trying to understand this special number, this special rule, on which all circles are based or formed – all circles, everywhere. And the more accurately they deduce it, the longer it gets. As Viv said, 3.142... has now been extended to millions of decimal places and doesn't look as if it's ever going to stop."

"So – it's a pretty sophisticated number. I guess that means it's quite recent, historically... say, from the time of Isaac Newton?" Yours truly trying to be clever again. And about to be shot down. Again.

"Well, actually, no. The first record of Pi is believed to be in the Egyptian 'Rhind' papyrus, dating from about 2000 BC. Archimedes worked on it about 250 BC, the Chinese from 200 to 500 AD, the Indians from about 500 AD, and Fibonacci in 1220 and Viète in 1593. Newton didn't get around to it until 1665."

"Wow – 2000 BC! So I guess there was an Egyptian foreman sucking in his breath and saying, 'Sorry squire, that'll take 30 cubits of gold thread to go around *that* column. Here are the figures.' "

"Hmmm." (There's that school-teachery look again – scares me to death.) "You should check out Fibonacci and Viète, sometime – their number theories are interesting."

John mumbles, "Yeah, some night when I can't sleep."

"As for the numbers after the decimal point, we shouldn't worry *too* much about how many, since a value of Pi to even 40 digits would be more than enough to compute the circumference of the Milky Way galaxy to an error less than the size of a proton." [20]

"Wow. Just what I needed last weekend. So, any other practical examples of Pi?"

Ellipses

"In 499, the Indian astronomer Aryabhata discovered that the orbits of the planets around the sun are ellipses, and published this in his book, the Aryabhatiya."

(Meanwhile in Britain we were wondering how the Romans had made that stuff that held blocks of stone together – or would we have to go back to sticks and mud. We went back to sticks and mud.)

"In the 17th century, Johannes Kepler wrote that the orbits along which the planets travel around the Sun are ellipses, and it became 'Kepler's First Law'. Isaac Newton included this as part of his law of universal gravitation."

"So, Newton nicked it. Melissa, can you give me an example?"

"Sure. To calculate the circumference of an ellipse:

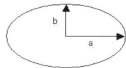

Approximate circumference of an ellipse :
Circumference = 2 * pi * sqrt((a^2+b^2)/2)"

"Thanks, Melissa."

Pi is obviously a fundamental rule in deciding both the *shape* and the *motion* of things within our universe. Which is all good stuff, because it means that Pi, along with calculus, will one day play a big part in getting our descendants to the other planets, and probably to other solar systems.

That Feeling...

But if you remember, I originally introduced Pi by saying, "How can such a 'messy' number be one of the fundamental rules of the universe?" Let's face it - one could understand if it was 3, or even 10 divided by 3, or even 42, but 3.14159... ?

So I think Pi can go into our melting pot, but I also think that we will be pulling it back out of the pot later. I don't think we're quite finished with Pi yet. I get the strangest feeling: all the authorities and egg-heads are whistling and looking the other way, while this strange thing has existed through all of eternity sitting there, looking innocent, but a constant reminder of... well, I don't know what. I honestly still want the universe to go tick-tock, to be fundamentally understandable, for all the pieces to fit together neatly... but the existence of this thing raises the hairs on the back of my neck.

Now, are there any other anomalies or fundamentals which we can track down - and understand without needing a PhD - which will be a help in trying to answer our original questions?

Chapter 8: The Golden Ratio

Melissa's explanation of Pi intrigued me so much that I wanted to track down other anomalies, and eventually I remembered Jimmy's reference to the golden ratio, in the Salford pub all those years ago.

As I read up on it, I realised that of all the topics in this book the golden ratio has possibly attracted more fanciful and fantastic notions then any other, in the long history of humankind (except perhaps for quantum physics in the last decade).

Which is another way of saying: 'Watch out for the nutters.'

It has been suggested that the golden ratio is contained in many things, from the shape of the Egyptian pyramids, to the shape of the human body.

You have only to search the Internet for ten minutes before you come across an enthusiast claiming that the golden ratio is "the basis for gravitation, and the tuning fork of God's Mind."

For this reason, I am going to try to deal with it in as clean and clinical a way as is possible. Still, the fact is that it 'exists'; and it could be deserving of just as much attention as Pi.

The ancient Greeks knew of the golden ratio from their investigations into geometry. Its discovery is usually attributed to Pythagoras (- that man again, the bane of my teenage years).

Ptolemy's theorem (Claudius Ptolemaeus 90-168 AD) is probably the easiest to understand:

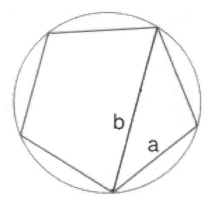

In a pentagram the ratio of the lines *a* to *b* is 1 : 1.618.

The golden ratio has been calculated to more than 1,050 decimal places [App1], but enough – I feel that headache coming on.

The Greeks loved to play games with such geometrical anomalies, and it has been suggested that the floor-plan and front elevation of the Acropolis are designed based on the golden ratio (?) :

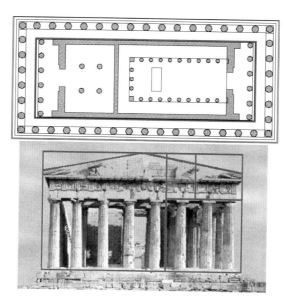

Leonardo Da Vinci also examined the golden ratio, and was interested in it as a basis for the shape of the human body.

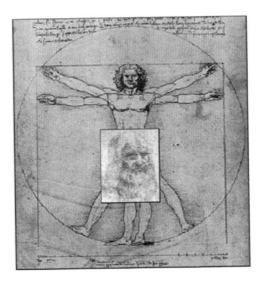

It is also *claimed* that Leonardo used the golden ratio as a basis for his works of art, including the Mona Lisa, and the Last Supper. (?) Good fun. And, of course, everyone loves a conspiracy.

In more modern times, as calculus and logarithms were explored, it was found that you could use the golden ratio to create a logarithmically perfect spiral: [21]

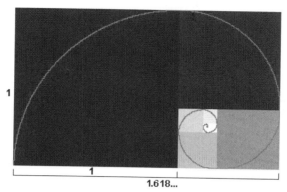

Draw a rectangle of length 1.618 and height 1, and divide off the square bit. In the new smaller rectangle on the right, divide off a new square. And keep repeating. Then join the 'dots' at the top of each dividing line.

As my friend Jimmy pointed out, the spiral now drawn describes the shape of the nautilus shell, and also many other shapes in nature.

Ok, so the golden ratio has been known since 325 BC, and is derived from two lines in a perfect pentagram. It was used by the Greeks in many of their designs, and it's been found in the structure of many objects in nature.

It's an 'irrational' number which seems to 'extend' into infinity, so it got my interest; but Jimmy, is it anything more than a mathematician's toy?

Still frowning am I, young grinning Buddha.

But hang on, who's this over here?

The Fibonacci Series

Oh dear, this guy looks like a real nerd. So why was such a fuss made about him?

Leonardo Fibonacci (1170 – 1250 AD) is attributed
with discovering what are now known as the
Fibonacci Numbers, or the Fibonacci Series.   [22]

While most of the civilised world (i.e. European white men) were sending their young and fair out to fight in the Crusades...

...No, hang on a minute... to fight the Moslems who had the temerity to live in their own countries and worship their own religions (how dare they!), and who had already worked out that the orbits of the planets were elliptical, when any right-thinking person knew full well that the Earth was flat...?

...Ok, ok, I'll stop there. Sorry about that.

Anyway – this young Italian's head was obviously in a different place. If not a different universe.

Fibonacci formed a numerical series starting from the numbers 0 and 1, by adding the last two numbers to get the next one:

0 + 1 = 1. 1 + 1 = 2. 1 + 2 = 3... and just keep on going.

Goodness knows why anyone would want to do this, but hey, that's mathematicians for you. And even *I* can understand the idea. It's *that* simple.

And what you get is the series of numbers shown below:

1, 2, 3, 5, 8, 13, 21, 34, 55, 89, 144, 233, 377, 610, 987...

(And I'm sure that for many of us the reaction to this revelation would be a big 'So what?')

Now, while this idea may look purely like yet another mathematical game, the Fibonacci Series is claimed to occur in nature in many different ways, including:

Rabbit reproductive cycles

Honeybees colony expansion

Plant growth [23]

Which makes me feel that this guy didn't get out a great deal.

My own personal interest in the Fibonacci series was piqued when I heard that it could be the foundation of the standard musical scale. [24]

All those years ago when I was learning the guitar and experimenting with harmonies and note-relationships, what I thought of as 'tuned', 'harmonic, 'pleasant' or 'natural' relationships between different musical notes in chords and harmonies apparently contained underlying 'Fibonacci-like' relationships. You know 'thirds', 'fifths', and 'octaves'? They really *are* relationships between firsts, thirds, fifths, and eighth notes in the scale, not just names. [App 2]

And the connection between the Fibonacci Series and the Golden Ratio? Well the Golden Ratio just 'exists in nature', doesn't it? And the Fibonacci Series is 'man-made', isn't it? So it was thought, but are you ready for this?: -

If we divide each number in the Fibonacci series by the number before it, we get a new series of numbers:

$$1/1 = 1, \quad 2/1 = 2, \quad 3/2 = 1.5, \quad 5/3 = 1.666,$$

$$8/5 = 1.6, \quad 13/8 = 1.625, \quad 21/13 = 1.61538$$

As we use bigger and bigger numbers from the Fibonacci series, the new generated number eventually settles down to 1.618 ! And 1.618 is, of course, the Golden Ratio. [App 3]

But hang on – I'm shaking my head, now. Surely the Fibonacci Series is just a man-made series of numbers. It can't possibly 'exist in nature', can it? How could that be? Aw, come on. This is just too bizarre. I'd need some other examples of the Fibonacci Series in nature before I could go along with that.

Whoops…

Helianthus   **Cone-flower**   **Pine Cone**

Many of the spiral arrangements in flowers and plants follow the Fibonacci series/golden-ratio formulae.

So we now seem to have two other 'fundamental' pieces of information that can go into our melting pot, the Golden Ratio and the Fibonacci series. Both appear to be rules of nature and, lo and behold, both also share the same attribute as Pi, in that they numerically 'go on forever'.

As I said before, for some reason, this is all making the hair stand up on the back of my neck. And I think that's because this is one of the few times in my life that wishing it wasn't so... (the universe turning out not to be quite as I thought it was) ...is not going to make a blind bit of difference.

Ok, that's enough playing with numbers. I'm hoping that later on these numeric sequences may have more meaning when we hold them up against the other contents of the melting pot.

The great thing about doing your own research is that you can shoot off at angles and change the subject of study, and no-one can tell you that you're wrong to do that. So now I want to look at 'life'....

Chapter 9: Snow In My Boots

"Life? Don't talk to me about Life."
- Marvin

Snow has crept over the top of my boots, and is melting inside. I'm tramping through a two-foot deep layer of snow in the hills of Hebden Bridge, following my older brother Peter – which I did seem to spend a lot of my early years doing. Not tramping through the snow, but following behind Peter.

He's a taciturn individual. Where the other three of us – two boys and a girl – would simulate human pogo sticks, he could always be found in a corner, reading a book, a faint look of disapproval on his face; or so we others thought. He became so immersed in his reading that you could stand at the side of him and talk for a full minute before he realised you were there. Our mother used to shout out, "Hey, unconscious!" at meal times - I think because she'd discovered that the trigger-word 'unconscious' brought him back into the real world. He rarely spoke, but some of those quiet, simple statements have stayed with me all my life.

Just now we've gone out for the day to visit his friends who live in a converted farm house – a whole bunch of people living what, for me, appears to be a pointless rural lifestyle, staying stoned most of the time and giving the impression that the Buddha was a complete beginner. Peter has obviously noticed that I feel out of place, my natural 24 year-old heavy-rock energy being at odds with the laid-back lifestyle around me. So he's taken me out for a walk through the snow. For miles.

The stone stairways down through Hebden Bridge are interesting – all set into the 45-degree hillside on which the town was built, and every step covered with a layer of ice. Interesting, but slow; and dangerous. Very 'coaches racing through the snow'; very 'The river's frozen hard; let's have a fair!'; very *not* funny.

Now we're out in the fields, negotiating our way around rocks taller than I am, and I can't see where we're supposed to be going. I'm ok with this, honestly I am. I'm serene. If Peter wants to do this then it's ok with me. If this is what Buddha-types do to get their kicks, then I too will simply look serene, and act as if I do this every other day. I am, of course, wearing a raincoat, a suit, and thin-soled stylish city boots; and of course no gloves. The air is completely still and unbelievably dry, and because sound hardly carries in these conditions I feel as if I'm in a bubble of reality that only extends around us by about ten feet. I could be on a planet that has never been touched by life.

Peter crouches, motions me over, and points down. Peeping through the hard packed snow is the tiniest blue flower I've ever seen. He looks at me, beaming, and quietly says, "Life will find a way."

Back at the farmhouse, watching my socks steam in front of the fire, I mention to him that life seems to me to be such an anomaly within the universe.

"Actually," he says, "I've always felt that life is more of an inevitability within the universe. Matter doesn't just support life – it seems to become life. That's just the way it is."

Another time I mentioned that I'd been reading about Zen Buddhism, and their main idea of 'enlightenment' – that it could come in a flash, at any moment. "What do you think?" I asked.

"Well," he drawled, "I've always felt that enlightenment was more of an ongoing process. Gradual."

I've found that over the years that one statement has allowed me to be a little more patient with myself, a little more forgiving.

*

The last moon mission brought back a piece of equipment which had been abandoned during the first mission, ten years before. Scientists decided to see exactly how 'sterile' the old equipment was, and took swabs from the inside surfaces. The life-forms that they found were re-grown in petrie-dishes, and it was determined that they were in fact… the common cold.

In the early days of NASA sterilisation was not thought to be a high priority, and a technician had sneezed inside the box before closing it.

What makes this story amazing is the fact that the equipment had been alternately baked and frozen as the Moon had turned its face toward and away from the Sun - one hundred and twenty times in the last 10 years, between a range of minus 250 degrees and plus 250 degrees - temperatures usually thought to be ideal for the complete sterilisation of microbes.

Halophiles are simple forms of life that can live in high salt concentrations such as The Great Salt Lake.

Methanogens, Acidophiles and Alkaliophiles can exist in highly concentrated chemical environments, dominant with methane, acids or alkalis.

Psychrophiles exist in extremely cold environments, such as the Arctic and the Antarctic.

Some tiny lifeforms (including fungi) have evolved to be able to live inside porous rocks, so long as they have moisture beneath and sunlight above.

*

The fact is, that it's very difficult to define what 'life' actually is. It can range from what appears to be no more than a simple chemical reaction, through to the highest life-form known – the creature typing these words.

Often, when I visit Wales, I stroll through one of the not-too-rugged woodland areas, and once I've stopped gawping at the carpets of bluebells I crouch down and brush aside the grass stems to take a closer look at what lies beneath. Even within a one-foot square of grass, the amount and variety of busy, scurrying life is staggering. It looks as if this planet is literally bursting with life at every possible opportunity; on every habitable surface, even in the tiniest gap. That small rock over there? Not only under it, but if it's even mildly porous then cleave it in half, and there's a good chance you'll find a chemical reaction going on inside.

It seems obvious, even to a school-child, that life, from microbes to spiders to humans, exploits every possible ecological niche. In other words, in whatever form is most appropriate, it expands to fill *any* available gap, whether it is spatial, social, or environmental.

Life, here on this planet, is not the exception; it is the rule.

Next time you look at a bunch of flowers, don't see the gardener's hard work, don't see the florist's merchandising; see Mother Nature's fireworks going off... in slow-motion.

Chapter 10: Growth and Fractals

"All art is but imitation of nature."
- Lucius Annaeus Seneca (Seneca the Younger)

"Although human subtlety makes a variety of inventions by different means to the same end, it will never devise an invention more beautiful, more simple, or more direct than does nature, because in her inventions nothing is lacking, and nothing is superfluous."
-Leonardo DaVinci

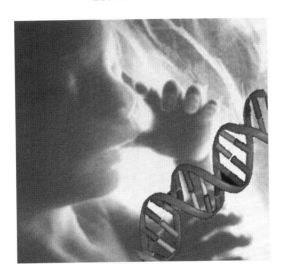

How many lifetimes would it take to understand life, nature, biology, and growth? A ridiculous question, of course – that particular path of enquiry will go on all the days of the human race.

That the drive and energy within nature is strong, is undeniable. That the yearning for survival and continuity is strong, is unquestionable.

Parents have been known to willingly die, so that their children survive. Were they *so* sure that the sacrifice would be worth it, that their children would be better people than they had been? I doubt that they even thought about it.

Nature, on all too many occasions, has allowed the mother to die in childbirth so that the child may survive. To nature, 'worth' and 'better' seem meaningless; 'continuity' and 'next' seem all-important.

Growth, survival, continuity – the unwritten, ingrained rules of the universe. It's difficult to know (in a philosophical sense) why that should be so important. But we just know that it is, and we feel very clearly *when* we're on the right track – every instinct inside us tells us that to protect and nurture young life is the right path.

So beyond that, I'm going to chicken out. (At least for now.)

Instead, I've been considering 'growth'. Growth in the sense of 'complexity'; growth in the sense of 'complicatedness'. I feel that it's important to take a look at how complex life is – something else that we usually take for granted. We all like to think of ourselves as complex organisms; it helps to bolster our 'sense of self' or 'sense of self-worth', and by extension we see *all* life as 'complex'.

Once again, I'd like to know if there is some sort of fundamental (-and of course I mean simple or basic) understanding that can be achieved so that we can understand the *process* of growth, and what that process requires.

Then I remembered something from ten years ago. Finally – one of my *own* skills can be brought into the mix! – computer programming.

Cue the audience to split their sides, and point derisively. Yes, I know, I know, I understand your reaction; and trust me, *I* have also laughed all these years. So many times I've heard programmers claim that they were near to achieving a 'synaptic-like object-orientated thinking-algorithm'. Well, we're still waiting, and we will wait for a very long time. The promise of artificial intelligence in computers has been a hollow one. Even the Head of Artificial Intelligence at MIT has ruefully declared that after 20 years of research they have now achieved a piece of software that has 'the intelligence level of a slow-witted slug'.

My understanding is this: that even as you read these words your brain is disconnecting old and creating new synaptic connections, from one moment to the next, as the information is absorbed, judged and stored. We do this every moment of our lives, and we're even able to retrieve a memory from years ago

- triggered by the simplest event, even a smell! That's how good the brain is. But it *has* had a few million years of practice.

No, what I'm talking about is 'growth', in the simplest sense.

I remembered that I'd written an algorithm (- a formula, a few lines of code) some years ago which generated a fractal pattern – which to put it simply, looks, on the computer screen, like something that has 'been grown'.

By the way, for those who don't know, a computer programmer's career development will usually follow these steps:
First: a program which prints "Hello World" and their name on the screen; don't ask me why – it's traditional.
Next: their own version of Tetris; to prove that they can.
Last: a Mandelbrot fractal generator.
After that, unless they go into 3D, it's all downhill.

So I dug out the code and updated it using a modern programming language, and ran it; and this appeared on the screen:

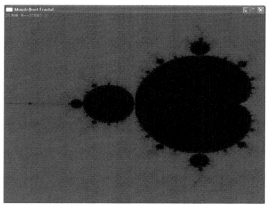

The whole fractal image

By now we've probably all seen Mandelbrot fractals (named after Benoît Mandelbrot, a French mathematician born 1924), but one of the interesting attributes of a fractal is that, if you get the formula right, and zoom in on a tiny segment, then there is no loss of detail. You can keep zooming in, and you just keep getting more detail – as if the fractal goes on into infinity.

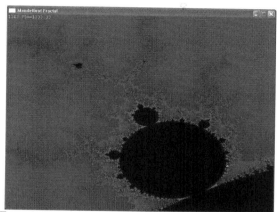
Zooming in on a tiny portion of the original fractal

"So," I hear you ask, "surely that needed a huge amount of programming code?" (– Well, you may not have, but you're going to get it anyway.)

Actually, no. Just 36 lines of code... and most of that code is used to stop the coloured pixels from going off the side of the screen, which can crash the program or even the computer. [App 4]

So what portion of that code is the 'growth code'? Just 3 lines, repeated again and again. [App 5] And I've even seen a *one-line* algorithm, written by someone else!

"A-hah," you say. "But that's only two dimensional. It's flat. Surely it would take a lot more to make it three dimensional?" Well actually, only one more line of code is needed to produce something like this:

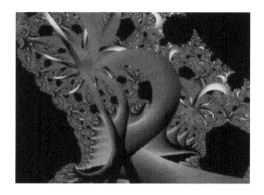

And of course then it's only a short hop to this:

Biologists are now suggesting that one possible way that DNA works is fractally, in a similar manner to that described above. Using fractals they can successfully 'model' and therefore (partially) explain complicated patterns in nature. In fact, the more they look at 'growth' the more a fractal process seems to be the only way to explain such complexity arising from such simplicity. [26] For example, the AAAS Journal says: "Fractal-like networks effectively endow life with an additional fourth spatial dimension... Organisms have evolved hierarchical branching networks... such as capillaries, leaves, mitochondria, and oxidase molecules." [28]

So it seems that the *principle* of growth that I've been looking for could be a very simple formula, repeated again and again...

which might account for this...

Acorn

...eventually becoming this.

Oak tree

and even more so, this...

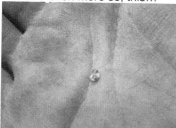

Sequoia seed

...eventually becoming this.

300ft Sequoia tree,
currently the largest living
organism on this planet

Conclusions:

The growth processes of life may be fractally based.

Fractals are tiny, simple pieces of information, repeated recursively, with incredible potential for expansion and growth.

Fractal information seems to 'extend' into infinity.

Addendum:

As a complete aside, and on a more humorous note just to finish off this section on growth, someone has suggested that

all Mandelbrot fractals contain the Fibonacci Series, as shown
by the relative size of the 'depressions' in the pattern:

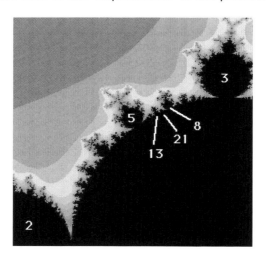

I know I didn't build it into *mine*. (Did I?)

*

And finally, next time you're at a party where the topic of
conversation turns to symbology (…don't they always!), you
might like to point out that

- the Caduceus of Hermes, officially known as the symbol for
  medicine since the early 16th century,

- which bears such an uncanny resemblance to DNA,
  discovered in 1953,

- was also the symbol for medicine in ancient Egypt!

Chapter 11: Summary So Far

It's time for a summary of what I feel I've found out so far. Remember the criteria that I've used?

I'm trying to answer the questions: What am I? Will I end?

I'm looking for information – even if that information is in the form of more questions – to put into the melting pot.

The information must *not* be based on 'faith', verbal gymnastics or my own wishful thinking.

Insofar as it is possible, I *will* use information from our scientific community (who after all are supposed to be the most advanced minds of our species), so long as I can dig out 'fundamental principles' that even I can understand.

I have also discovered that there are 'anomalies' in this universe which the scientific community make use of, but otherwise cannot explain.

Let's see if I can list what I've found:

It's not possible to examine these main questions by so-called conventional means. The body and brain are explicable in terms of normal biological mechanics; but the mind, life, 'being', is not explicable by normal means.

There are anomalies in this universe – mysteries, enigmas, call them what you will – which mathematics *has* uncovered.

These anomalies appear to be fundamental rules underlying the universe – they've always been there, we're just in the process of defining and understanding them (and looking for others).

Pi, the golden ratio, the Fibonacci series; all these (and others) seem to be totally irrational numbers, and to disappear into infinity. As do fractals.

Life, rather than existing separately from matter, may well be an inevitable consequence *of* matter.

The growth process of life may be fractally based, and as such subject to mathematical rules.

We seem to have precious few tools in our armoury, other than our minds, our imaginations, and, because we know our imaginations can be a little unruly, the (self-)disciplines of science and mathematics.

Stop checking your watch – it's not time to go yet! Woah! - Sit back down there at the back!

Trust me – if it was going to be difficult then I'd be the first one out of here. I can just about handle the right-angled triangle, and the inverse square law (-oh yeah, that's another unexplained phenomenon), but anything further and the migraine kicks in.

I *do* promise that I will keep it as simple as possible, with as many illustrations as possible. I haven't the *least* interest in anything even remotely complex. Let's leave the really hard stuff to the big-brains; after all, what we're looking for are the *fundamental* principles underlying what they have found.

What *we* need to have is the willingness to try to absorb the fundamentals, and at the same time the sophistication to appreciate the big picture.

What's the worst thing that can happen?

We might find some answers?

It is my conviction that pure mathematical construction enables us to discover the concepts and the laws connecting them, which gives us the key to the understanding of nature ... In a certain sense, therefore, I hold it true that pure thought can grasp reality, as the ancients dreamed.
-     Albert Einstein, 1933

Chapter 12: The Road Ahead

The most beautiful sensation to appreciate is the mystic.
He to whom the emotion is strange, who no longer
wonders and stands in awe, is as good as dead.
- Albert Einstein

When beginning any journey, we need to be well equipped for the road ahead. We need to be very clear where we're starting from, and have as clear an idea as possible of where we're going. We need to be very aware what tools and provisions we will need along the way, and also what may constitute excess baggage and slow us down, or even prevent us from getting there.

Here are some of those things that I would like to draw to your attention:

Nomenclature

Classification, categorisation and labelling.   In other words, the descriptive terms that we use.

Both in this book, and in real life, I have been reticent to use words such as 'God', 'spirit', 'afterlife', 'dimensions', 'belief', since the biggest fault with such general purpose words – and I cannot emphasize this enough – is that people *always* respond with an attitude of: "I know what you mean by that." When, in fact, they don't.

This has happened *so* many times in my discussions with people that I'd say that it's the biggest impediment to communication, learning and mutual understanding – at least in these more esoteric subjects - between people.

As a recent example, I spent a very pleasant afternoon with my mother (who is not normally the most forth-coming of people) and finally, after five decades, and after she'd fed me, I chose the right moment to ask her what she 'really thought'. Well, she is near the end of her life, whereas I am - I hope – at the middle of mine; possibly I should have asked her sooner, but better now that not at all.

Inevitably, being a born and bred Catholic, my mother used the word 'God'. It took another four hours of patient discussion for me to realise that, contrary to my life-long assumption, she did not mean God in the traditional Catholic sense - not the old man with the white beard who sits on the clouds and remains completely separate from humanity - but her own personal vision was of a single universal entity which encompasses literally everything, and of which we are all *already* a part. Wow!

She still goes to church every Sunday, though. Some habits are hard to break.

Consider the words 'spirituality' and 'metaphysics'. In most day-to-day conversations both words will elicit an immediate belittling response from the listener, because to the majority of people they signal the fact that the person using them has given up their capacity for judgment for a 'quick mental fix' – a surrender to a particularly narrow faith or belief.

Whereas the problem may well be that the language – English in particular – simply does not contain terms which are appropriate to what is being described.

As humankind grows we will need new terms. Inevitably we will continue to use and refine old terms for the purpose, as we have done before; but I would ask two things:

Be patient with people; spend the time. Find out what they *really* mean, and possibly, between the two of you, find alternate words for what you are both trying to describe.

If at all possible, re-use old words, or preferably invent new words, to describe elements of this tricky subject matter.

For example, more and more I find I am using the word 'essence' instead of 'spirit'. While it may be a little more subtle and need more explanation, at least, as a term, it is not quite so loaded with preconceived connotations.

Respect

Listen, listen, and listen again. Remind yourself that there is a whole other being behind those eyes. Just like you. A being with hopes and fears and dreams, just like yours. A being who has struggled with everything that life has thrown at them, just as you have.

Listen to how they got here. Listen to what they went through on the way. Respect where they're 'coming from', and how they have arrived at the conclusions they're expressing. Make no mistake - because every human's life is different, with different challenges and different lessons learned - they *will* have something that you can learn.

And you know who I'm lecturing on this particular subject, don't you.
The biggest culprit. Myself.

Tools Of Perception

There were once societies that disdained even the use of writing: the Celts and the Native Americans in particular, who felt that the only 'pure' way to pass on information and history was verbally - that any other way would corrupt what was being told or taught.

Later, both the telescope and the microscope were called 'instruments of the devil', even though, what could be more 'natural' than reflected or refracted light?

I still use paper and pencil to balance my home accounts, but only because I long ago realised that I'm actually number-dyslexic (if I read four numbers in a row, when I get to the fourth my mind erases the first three), and so the calculator between my ears needs all the workouts I can give it. For other jobs I will, of course, use the most appropriate tool for the job, which in the case of writing this book, is my computer. My grandfather would have been horrified that I was not using a fountain pen. My great-grandfather would have used a quill.

The point is, that even though we try to hang on to what we are familiar with, eventually we have to admit that better tools for the job have arrived. Instead of burning people at the stake, or bleeding them with leeches for their own good, we now totally accept that – for the most part – psychiatry and psychotherapy are better tools for the job.

And so it is with science, and mathematics.

Science, as we have seen through 'the scientific method', is, at it's heart, a method of observing, hypothesizing, and testing, until a common theorem or guideline can be found, which can then be used by anyone, anywhere, and will always be true enough to save a child's life or help to irrigate a field.

Mathematics, on the other hand, is *a way of looking at existence*. A way of attempting to perceive the unperceivable. The crystalline molecular structure of carbon was mathematically predicted long before any electron microscope saw the beautiful lattice-like arrangement of the atoms. [29]

Mathematics is the regular tool of physicists who bang elementary particles together. The way they make sense of their results is through mathematics.

Mathematics is now also showing the potential of being able to reach into areas of thinking and judgment that the 'standard' sciences cannot.

We, as the diggers and baby-makers or our society, do not need to understand the complexities or subtleties of such a discipline, or be able to undertake the rigours of such work; our shamans already do that for us. We just need to be able to judge the accumulated findings, and to make some human sense of them.

And so often it's us, and not the shamans, who are better at that.

'The analysis of data will not by itself produce new ideas.'
- Edward de Bono

So don't be afraid of maths. It's just a tool; a way of thinking, a way of perceiving. Probably the most revolutionary tool that the upright hominid has invented since Galileo put one lens in front of the other and said, "Well… will you just look at that! Damn – she's closed her curtains. Never mind, where's the moon?"

Imagination

Imagination:-

That which sets us apart from the other species on this planet.

That which will take us to the stars.

That, with which, we will find the answers we seek.

The Narrow View

A man stood on the shore, looking out to sea. "There," he said, pointing, "is the edge of the world." And he was wrong.

His grandson stood in the middle of a great plane and said, "See, the Earth is flat." Little realizing that Eratosthenes had calculated that the Earth was spherical, and had also calculated its diameter, 2000 years before.

The Vatican stood in the centre of the universe, and forbad anyone else to stand anywhere else, either. If you questioned that fact, they would prove to you that you were wrong. Permanently. Or in smaller stages, until you agreed.

A man stood on the edge of the universe and said, "The universe is expanding; therefore it came from a single point. And therefore, before that there was nothing." Pardon? Without leaving the planet you were born on? Without being able to see beyond the horizon? Even while knowing that our most elementary and basic understandings of our surroundings change from one generation to the next? Then his peers proved his basic tenet wrong, but they all agreed to keep quiet about it.

A man stood in the middle of a stage and said, "We have weighed the universe, and the result does not agree with what we can see. Therefore, there must be some sort of invisible substance out there, that we cannot see. We shall henceforth call it Phlogiston… oh no, sorry, wrong sheet, …Dark Matter."

And lo, in the fullness of time, the high priest, Patrick Moore, asked a junior priest, "Do you *believe* in Dark Matter?" and on hearing that word all the little people hid their faces in their hands and wept that the tools that they had spent generations sharpening were being dulled by the Media.

> *"Belief gets in the way of learning."*
> - Robert Heinlein

As thinking beings we can *not* afford to have a narrow view, a bigoted view. While making the best possible tools, we must maintain the broadest possible outlook, and be prepared to be adaptable.

We all love the applause of our fellow creatures; we all like the idea of inspiring awe in others. But at what cost – to them, and to ourselves?

We would all love to have, or to give, absolute answers. But better to listen, to continue learning, and to be prepared to say, "This is our knowledge so far."

Otherwise, we risk being a laughing stock to each other.

We risk ignorance.

We risk losing the ability to learn.

(Yes, it is a lovely pulpit, isn't it. I'm glad you like it. I got it second-hand; it polished up a treat!)

New Ways Of Thinking

In considering the questions of existence, we need new ways of thinking; not 'we' as a group necessarily, but 'we' as individuals. The way that each of us personally thinks.

This is not a box of Lego we're dealing with, after all. This is not a Rubik's Cube that we know ultimately has a solution.

A better simile would be that we are each a small jigsaw piece in a huge jigsaw. Trying to see the whole picture. If we are not able to, then at least that simile may help us to be gentler and more forgiving with ourselves.

The understanding of the big picture may not, in fact, be possible; but we cannot stop trying. And that fact alone tells us something very important about what we are.

But we *will* need to think differently in order to undertake the task. We *will* need to exercise our minds in ways that we never have before, in order to develop the mental strength and suppleness required to absorb and evaluate new ideas and information.

Disagreements?

I said earlier: "Respect where they're 'coming from', and how they have arrived at the conclusions they're expressing. Make no mistake - because every human's life is different, with different challenges and different lessons learned - they *will* have something that you can learn.

And I meant it.

I'm not setting myself up as 'a learned one'. The very thought makes me dissolve into laughter. ("He's making it up as he goes along!" -The Life Of Brian). Too right, pal. We're *all* feeling our way, here. We're *all* learning as we go. And we *can* learn from each other.

I have to admit that for too many years, even within this society rather than on the top of a mountain, I took the attitude that 'solitary' learning was somehow better (– I won't actually say that I thought no-one could teach me anything).

Luckily, these last few years the universe has got its own back on me. An idea explained, a chance remark, some-else's viewpoint (thanks, Sandy), a mirror held up (thanks, Liz); and suddenly some of the pieces fall into place. You didn't even know they were *out* of place! Suddenly the eyes go wide, the jaw drops, if you're lucky your eyes fill with tears.

So…

If you know something I don't know – then let me know.

If I've been inaccurate on any point – then say so.

Ultimately, we're all in this together.

Chapter 13: Revelations

Pi Revisited

Remember how I said that Pi and the golden ratio were such 'messy' numbers to be rules of the universe? You'd expect 'perfect' numbers, wouldn't you? You'd expect – somehow – beauty?

After a while I thought I'd better do a little more (ahem) research into these fiddly numbers. So I gritted my teeth, got a fresh double-strength cup of coffee; cigs and ashtray ready...

And what I found literally made my jaw drop:

$$\frac{2}{\pi} = \frac{\sqrt{2}}{2} \frac{\sqrt{2 + \sqrt{2}}}{2} \frac{\sqrt{2 + \sqrt{2 + \sqrt{2}}}}{2} \cdots$$

"What the hell is *that*!?" I shouted.

Remember that Pi is supposed to be 3.142... etc

It seems that François Viète, who Melissa mentioned earlier, had taken a fresh look at Pi - and this is the point - stopped thinking about it in straight decimal form, and had come up with this formula. But of course, this is what mathematics, and mathematicians, are good for! They look at things in a completely different way; from a completely different viewpoint. Here was the beauty and the symmetry that I always felt Pi should have!

Then I felt *completely* stupid: How could I possibly have thought that the universe functioned in decimal? How human-centric is that! Duh – caught out again, when I should be old enough to know better.

Then a thought: Is this revelation recent?

No. François came up with this in 1593! Why had nobody mentioned this before? It's been known for *that* long?

Then a slight shiver. Once more, the game's afoot!

Are there any more like that? Yes...

$$\frac{2}{1} \cdot \frac{2}{3} \cdot \frac{4}{3} \cdot \frac{4}{5} \cdot \frac{6}{5} \cdot \frac{6}{7} \cdot \frac{8}{7} \cdot \frac{8}{9} \cdots = \frac{\pi}{2}$$

(Wallis's Proof)

And my personal favourite (because it's easy to remember and so you can bore people with it at parties):

$$\frac{1}{1} - \frac{1}{3} + \frac{1}{5} - \frac{1}{7} + \frac{1}{9} - \cdots = \frac{\pi}{4}$$

(Liebniz' Proof)

All beautiful. All symmetrical. And all going on forever.

Though I'm still not too happy about that last bit – 'forever'. The words 'carpet' and 'finger-nails' spring to mind again.

But what about the golden ratio?

The Golden Ratio Revisited

Why am I now not surprised? Remember that the golden ratio was 1.618... in decimal form? Here are two alternate forms of the golden ratio (represented by the Greek letter 'phi')

$$\phi = 1 + \cfrac{1}{1 + \cfrac{1}{1 + \cfrac{1}{1 + \cdots}}}$$

$$\phi = \sqrt{1 + \sqrt{1 + \sqrt{1 + \sqrt{1 + \cdots}}}}$$

- again showing the beauty and the symmetry that I always felt should be there.

To be absolutely honest, I'm not sure *what* I've found here. But somehow it feels incredibly important. *Am I* looking at some fundamental rules of the universe? For some reason this new symmetry makes that possibility seem all the more likely.

I have to remind myself – these have *always* been here functioning quietly, determining shape, motion, and growth – part of the cogs and gears mechanism of the tick-tock universe. If all life in the universe disappeared tomorrow they would go on functioning just the same.

It's only recently that we humans have noticed them, named them, tagged them, and pretended that they were our own.

Chapter 14: Flexing Mental Muscles

Learn as if you were going to live forever.
Live as if you were going to die tomorrow.
- Mahatma Gandhi

During my journey I began to realise that I was constantly coming up against the limits of my own long-held belief systems. I had a choice: either I could ignore the fact that the universe was not conforming to my comfortable views of how it should behave and just blather on to justify my own misconceptions, or I could really make an effort to bend my brain into understanding the new ideas that I was discovering. Remember, here you have a man who agonises over the mysteries of the universe while lying full-length on a sofa, smoking yet another cigarette. It became painfully obvious that I would have to 'make an effort' – ugh – something I've avoided all my life. And in order to do that, I would have to exercise my brain. When did I last do that? When did I last *really* have to get my head around a totally new idea? Probably decades ago! Children do this all the time. For them, every day is a stream of new ideas and revelations that must be quickly absorbed. As adults, most of us have developed the habit of absorbing an idea (if we must) then quickly switching off our brains again.

'Flexing mental muscles' – how? I always felt that crosswords or Mensa tests were particularly pointless wastes of time, but maybe that's just me. So in order to delay the inevitable (-actual mental work) I went looking for early examples of flexible thinkers, and was quite pleasantly surprised.

We tend to think of generations earlier than our own as being very wedded to narrow points of view, and very rigid in their mindsets. Undoubtedly this was true for many people in the Victorian age; they developed conformism to a fine art probably never seen before, or since. Ladies willingly strapped themselves into bodices so tight that they were permanently on the verge of fainting. Men went marching (strolling, actually) into battle in bright red jackets, which effectively said, 'Here I am. Machine-gun me.' All because of a strange society-wide notion that conformity equalled stability equalled safety (at least for the society, if not the individual).

But even within that society a number of people were very quietly laying the foundations for new ways of thinking and reasoning. Charles Dickens, Charles Darwin, Mark Twain, the Curies; all the Victorian writers, engineers, physicists, biologists, and chemists who attempted to view the world in a different way. (I wouldn't include Lewis Carroll since it's well known that he was as high as a kite and away with the fairies most of the time, which is where his 'insightful' stories came from.)

So when did 'flexing mental muscles' really begin? We tend to think of classical Greece, the birthplace of democracy. Greece *was* democratic, one man one vote; so long as that voter was a man, and not a woman, poor, a slave, or a tradesman. Even so, Greece laid a foundation which later began to rise again after the French Revolution, which in turn affected the American Revolution, the Russian Revolution, and the rise of socialism in Great Britain.

Into our tight-corseted Victorian world Edwin Abbott published the first edition of 'Flatland', a light-hearted story about the occupants of a completely 2-dimensional world.

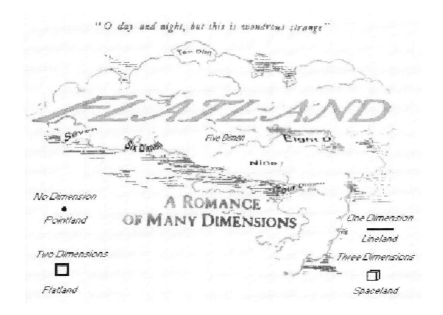

"Imagine a vast sheet of paper on which straight Lines, Triangles, Squares, Pentagons, Hexagons, and other figures, instead of remaining fixed in their places, move freely about, on or in the surface, but without the power of rising above or sinking below it, very much like shadows -- only hard with luminous edges -- and you will then have a pretty correct notion of my country and countrymen." [30]

Besides being a well-observed commentary on Victorian society, the essence of the story is that the hero is visited by one of the inhabitants of 'Spaceland', who appears to him as a gradually increasing circle.

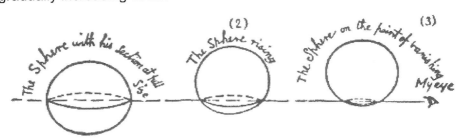

Abbott's original sketch of the visit.

The hero realises that there are other dimensions ('Spaceland'), but in trying to explain this to his people he is imprisoned for his heresy.

So with Abbot, and others, as our inspiration, it's now time for our own mental exercises. Here are a couple I found:

Mental Exercise 1

Place your fingertips down on a tabletop.
Imagine that the tabletop is Flatland.
Imagine the occupants of Flatland observing that there are 5 new individuals entering their country, whereas *you* know it is only one.
Imagine their bafflement as you remove your fingertips.

Don't give me *that* look. Let's be honest between us – most people never actually exercise either their bodies or their brains beyond what they know they are *already* capable of achieving. And I may be (heaven forbid) asking you to use your brain in a way that you never have before. Otherwise, what's the point? Go on – give it another try.

Mental Exercise 2

Imagine a 4-dimensional being entering our 3 dimensional world.
Would it look like a 3-dimensional object?
As it entered or exited, what would that behaviour or movement look like to us?

Don't worry too much if you had trouble with the second exercise.
The fact is, that because our bodies and brains are literally built in, and exist in, 3 dimensions it is virtually impossible for any human being to imagine anything greater than 3 dimensions.
Our cognitive abilities are based mainly on our perceptive faculties – we see length, breadth and width. We spend our earliest years learning about distance, collisions, balance, spatial relationships – these of course are completely necessary for survival, but guarantee that we inevitably develop quite rigid styles of thinking.

It's interesting that many of the Zen koans (poems) are deliberately designed to shake this complacency – to give the mind 'a good kicking'. Of course the effectiveness of these is in direct proportion to the listener's willingness to *be* kicked, to assimilate new ideas and new ways of thinking. Or not.

Even so, we *are* very inventive, imaginative creatures, and if we find that our 'sight' is limited, then we *will* invent some new means of perception.

Perhaps it's by closing one eye and squinting, or inventing the optical telescope, or inventing the electron microscope, or by constructing huge infra-red astronomy dishes; or – in the situation that we now find ourselves – creating a whole new way of thinking about things, a whole new angle of perception towards existence, a whole new way of viewing what we've always taken for granted, called Mathematics.

Mental Exercise 3: Imagine

Imagine a point:	○
Stretch the point into a line: A line forms when a point is extended in a particular direction.	
Stretch the line into a square: Shifting the line at right angles to its length generates a square.	
Stretch the square into a cube: Moving the square at right angles to its plane produces a cube.	
Stretch the cube into a hyper-cube: Moving the cube at right angles to all three previously defined directions creates a hypercube.	

No, I'm sorry. I was doing just fine until that last one. (Where's the paracetamol?)

I've tried and I've tried, and I just *can't* do it. I can't imagine a hypercube. The illustration above is, after all, a fake – merely a way of saying 'it would have *this* many surfaces' without actually being able to show it accurately.

It is actually a 2D drawing representing a 3D shape – which is a clever trick anyway, we monkeys are quite good at that. But after we've 'built' the 3D shape in our minds we're then asked to take it one step further and pretend that it's 4D!

I can't imagine more than 3 dimensions – at least not in the sense of a physical object like a cube. But hang on – I've just remembered…

"Mathematicians can define a **point**." Well, ok, I can accept that – it doesn't sound too difficult. We don't need to see the maths, I guess. If I remember, you just define it as a two value co-ordinate, such as x and y.	°
"Mathematics can be used to define a **line**." I can accept that too – I know from my programming days that you only need 4 numbers to define a line, usually labelled x1,y1, x2,y2.	
"Mathematics can be used to define a **square**." 4 pairs of co-ordinates now, one to define each corner: (x1,y1), (x2,y2), (x3,y3), (x4,y4)	
"Mathematics can be used to define a **cube**." By doing just more of the same, I guess.	
"Mathematics can be used to define a hypercube." [31]	
- Say what??!!	

But, *of course.* Mathematics *is* not just a tool for measuring and perception, but *also* a method of description.

Mathematics *can* describe a 4 dimensional object in absolute detail, in the same way that 3-dimensional, 2-dimensional, and 1-dimensional objects can be described.

So, does this mean that 'greater than 3-dimensional' things exist?

Who knows? But if they do, then our only hope of 'seeing' them is through mathematics, our 'new microscope'.

My understanding – and I have to stress that this is *my* understanding (feel free to check into this yourself) – is that as mathematicians explore the higher levels of maths a very strange thing happens: the equations do not balance *unless* extra dimensions are taken into account.

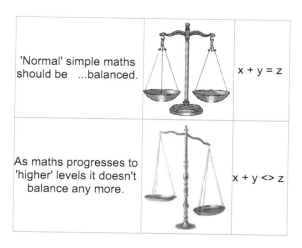

'Normal' simple maths should be ...balanced.		$x + y = z$
As maths progresses to 'higher' levels it doesn't balance any more.		$x + y <> z$

Here is a quote from Scientific American which may give you a flavour:

"This theory [to unite all physical interactions] called N=8 supergravity--is the maximally symmetric theory possible in four dimensions and it has been a subject of intense research since the 1980s." [32]

In other words, in searching for a new theory of gravity, i.e. an understanding of gravity that 'ties it in' with everything else instead of thinking of it as 'separate', physicists and mathematicians simply *have* *to* allow for more than 3 dimensions in their calculations.

Important Point

Let's remind ourselves: mathematics is just a tool, like a ruler. It doesn't actually 'do' anything by itself. But it *is* used by all the other disciplines such as engineering, physics, even biology, to measure and to understand *their* own results.

So maybe it's time to check out what the physicists have found… and a quick search for 'extra dimensions' immediately turns up –

SCIENTIFIC AMERICAN

Extra dimensional theories are claimed to work in 10 or 11 dimensions.

Moshe Rozali, a physicist at the University of British Columbia, explains.

These numbers seem to be singled out in the search for a fundamental theory of matter. The more you probe the fundamental structure of matter, the simpler things seem to become. In developing new theories that can encompass the current ones, scientists look for more simplicity in the form of symmetry. In addition to being elegant, symmetry is useful in constraining the number of competing models. The more symmetry there is, the fewer models that fit that symmetry exist.

- and there is such a proliferation of similar information throughout the physics community, and around the web, as to make one realise that this is now established theory; the assumption being that everyone knows about it.

"Although the human mind comprehends the universe with three spatial dimensions, some theories in physics, including string theory, include the idea that there are additional spatial dimensions. Such theories suggest that there may be a specific number of spatial dimensions such as 10."

"All string theories include the idea of a hyperspace of more than three spatial dimensions." [33]

Woah! String theory - what's that? The cause or root, maybe, of these extra dimensions? Now *that* rings a bell.

Time for another dash down memory lane,
then a little catching up with more recent discoveries…

Chapter 15: Comets, Girls and Apples

The Big

"Dad! Dad!"

There are very few sounds guaranteed to bring this somnolent human being from horizontal to vertical without apparent visible help, except for maybe "We've got free tickets for 'Yes'." and "This cream cake's yours."
But, "Dad! Dad!" will always do it.

I then continued the last few feet to the front door of our house with apparent nonchalance, since it doesn't do to let them see you fuss too much.
"It's there! It's there!" 12-year-old Sonia was bouncing up and down, and pointing at the sky. "The comet! I saw it first!"

It was one of those rare moments when you look, and think, 'It's true… somehow I thought it was just an idea - just a picture in a book…'

Even when it isn't raining in Manchester (-some say their granddad described such a mythological time), the whole region has incredibly damp air and constant cloud cover, which is why the American colonies sent cotton here to be spun into thread in an atmosphere which would help the cotton fibres cling together without breaking. Consequently astronomy is not a high art, or even, most of the time, an option. We were very lucky to have a cold clear March night to view the comet.

"It doesn't look very big."
"Probably smaller than the moon, but bigger than our house."
"Wooh."
(We later found out that comet Hale-Bop was over two billion miles away, beyond the orbit of Jupiter, which made it probably the most visible comet of all time.)
"Why does it have a tail, Dad?"
"Well, it's made up of ice, maybe a little rock, but mainly ice, and the Sun's light and heat cause the ice to heat up and steam away, so that the long tail always points away from the Sun."
"Will we see it again?"
"Not in our lifetimes."
"So where does it go?"
So it was time to remind Sonia about the Sun as the centre of the Solar System, and how the planets and other debris orbit the Sun because of gravitational pull. Sonia had already played a computer game called 'Damocles' where she could land on different planets, and she had a pretty good idea of the Ecliptic Plane. But tonight brought the reality that bit closer.

After our evening meal we had our feet up, righting the wrongs of the world (-mainly school), expressing indignation at the injustices in the world (-mainly school), and discussing how the lot of humankind could be improved (-by not going to school).
"They were teaching us about atoms today."

"Oh, yeah?" - this was at a time when science was still taught in school - "how was it?"

"I don't think the teacher quite understood it."

"Ah. I see. Shall I go over it?"

Sonia's reaction was the fractionally raised single eyebrow and the slightly pursed lips which said, 'Oh well. If you must.' I really don't know where she learns such expressions.

"Come on, kiddo. It's easier than Astronomy."

"Ok."

The Small

"The ancient Greeks had an idea that everything was made up of atoms – the word *is* actually Greek – tiny particles that combined together in different combinations could make up people, comets, and err… apples."

"Back then? Clever. How did they know?"

"They didn't know for sure. They just thought that it was the only possible way that a complex thing like a stone or a person *could* be formed – from tiny particles. And of course that would even explain water, different particles more loosely connected, which would flow and bend around objects."

"So when were atoms really discovered?"

"It was an idea that grew over the centuries, then when scientists began to combine chemicals together to make new substances it became obvious that the theory was fairly correct. John Dalton really nailed it down in 1808 when he described how Carbon could be combined with Oxygen to make Carbon Monoxide and Carbon Dioxide, and Hydrogen and Oxygen go together to make water."

"So how many types of atoms are there?"

"About a hundred or so in nature, which we usually call the Periodic Table, but being clever little monkeys we've managed to create some entirely new ones by smacking the old ones pretty hard."

"Ok, dad, you've always taught me to be sceptical about what I can't see. Why should I believe this?"

"Well, apart from the fact that different elements *can* be combined, as predicted by atomic theory, into new chemicals – for example, into new kinds of plastic… here's a picture taken by an electron microscope of a lattice of carbon atoms all joined up and holding hands."

"Cool! But why carbon?"

"Because carbon's one of the most common elements on this planet, and it just loves to get together with other carbon atoms in different combinations and groupings – everything from pencil lead to diamonds - or with other atoms to form new chemicals, or even little girls."

"Huh?"

"Yep. Most of your body has carbon in it, in a variety of combinations with oxygen and hydrogen." I think at that point Sonia wanted to take a bath.

"So…", that little smirk again, "what are atoms made of?" That's my girl!

"Ok – it's not too difficult, but maybe I'd better draw some diagrams."

"Ok. Let's take the apple you're eating. You can take a bite out of it because your teeth separate the atoms from each other.

So the whole apple is made up of atoms closely packed together.

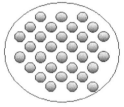

Now, each atom appears to have a centre, called a nucleus, and an outer shell...

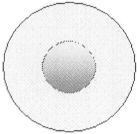

The nucleus actually contains Protons and Neutrons; the shell is made up of Electrons that spin around the Nucleus so fast that they appear to be solid."

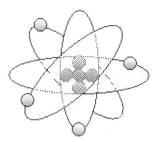

"Hey – they spin around just like the planets around the Sun."

"Yes. Nature repeats *that* design many times over, from electrons around atoms, to moons around planets, to planets around solar systems, to solar systems whizzing around the galaxy."

"So - what's the smallest thing there is?"

"Oh. I don't know. My friend Tony used to say that one day they would discover the ultimate smallest particle; but I wasn't so sure that it was that simple…"

*

Ten years later (I told you I was busy) I got time to go into this question, and found out that it's now known that protons and neutrons contain 'Quarks':

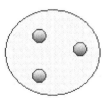

And electrons and quarks contain 'Strings'.

So 'strings' (sometimes called 'superstrings') are the lowest level that they've been able to detect so far – so low level that they are not even discreet 'particles' anymore! More like 'forces' having no actual dimensions…

'All string theories include the idea of a hyperspace of more than three spatial dimensions. The "extra" spatial dimensions are theoretically "compact" or "collapsed" dimensions. This means that they are not as extended in space as the three familiar spatial dimensions. The collapsed dimensions are too small to observe directly.' [34,35]

Personal Opinion

I came across the idea of multi-dimensions some time ago, and I remember thinking, "Yes, but what could those other dimensions actually be? Because the 'usual' 3 dimensions are *already* concerned with spatial connections – the others must be concerned with different sorts of 'connectivity' altogether." But it seems as if physicists cannot easily free themselves from old dogmas, since they so often say:

'The "extra" spatial dimensions are theoretically "compact" or "collapsed" dimensions. This means that they are not as extended in space as the three familiar spatial dimensions. The collapsed dimensions are too small to observe directly.'

Whenever I read about strings and the extra dimensions I hear the same thing: that the other dimensions are 'collapsed' or 'too small to see'. The scientists obviously still prefer to think of them as 'spatial' dimensions. I think that these extra dimensions are, in fact, concerned with a completely different sort of connectivity. I will be returning to this point at the end.

To continue, quarks and strings are described as existing at 'Quantum level'. What other 'levels' are there?

'Molecular' level	- Groups of atoms, which together make a molecule, e.g. Hydrogen and Oxygen make water.
'Atomic' level	- Atoms, e.g. individual elements such as Carbon and Oxygen
'Subatomic' level	- Electrons, Protons, Neutrons

Ok, got it:
- me (and apples) are made of molecules
- molecules are made of atoms
- atoms are made of electrons, protons and neutrons
- and those tiny particles are made of quantum level stuff

Hmmm.
Time to find out what's happening at quantum level…

Chapter 16: Down the Rabbit Hole

Reality is not only stranger than we suppose, but stranger than we can suppose.
-J. B. S. Haldane

If quantum mechanics hasn't profoundly shocked you, you haven't understood it yet.
- Niels Bohr

Wow. How to describe this? Quantum Mechanics (to give it it's full title) is a field of study which attempts to unravel and explain what is actually going on at sub-atomic level.

Why? Because things down there don't make any sense.

One simple example is that if we were to apply Newtonian (planetary and apple) theory, and Maxwellian (electric motor) theory to electrons, then electrons *should* simply collapse into the nucleus of the atom, instead of happily spinning around it. And obviously they don't. So at this incredibly low level the forces involved seem to be acting very differently to the ones that we take for granted in our larger 'everyday' world of planets, girls, and apples.

One of the most profoundly shocking examples has been 'quantum-entanglement'. Let me describe it:

One photon (-literally one very basic particle) is split into two.

One of the two is given 'spin', via a filter,
and the other reacts as if it has also been spun.

Even though they are both now physically separate objects!

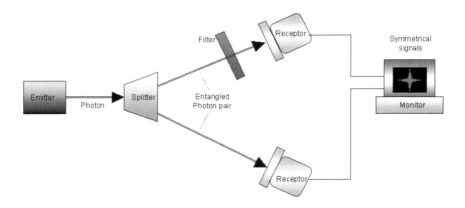

When this finally sank in with me I cannot tell you how much I laughed. In one fell swoop one of the greatest assumptions in physics, not to mention the thinking of humankind, had been overturned – that all objects and particles exist as completely separate entities.

Let's hear from the people who have been doing this quantum-level research:

"When the original photon splits into two photons, the resulting photon pair is considered entangled.
To illustrate, if an entangled photon meets a vertical polarizing filter the photon may or may not pass through. If it does, then its entangled partner will not because the instant that the first photon's polarization is known, the second photon's polarization will be the exact opposite. [37]
Whatever happened to one particle would thus immediately affect the other particle, wherever in the universe it may be. Einstein called this "Spooky action at a distance." [38]
- Amir D. Aczel, Entanglement, The Greatest Mystery In Physics

When Einstein called this "Spooky action at a distance" he was admitting that this phenomenon broke all previously understood rules. Calling something "spooky" doesn't mean that you understand it, it means that you *don't* understand it and *can't* explain it, and furthermore it breaks all the rules of your personal reality.

I said earlier, as part of The Scientific Method, "and let everybody else check it" –and that's exactly what has been happening. Even NASA: 'For this example, when one particle goes through the double slit, its twin also undergoes a ghost interference pattern even though it never went through a slit.' **[39]**

You're probably wondering by now, even though this is all very interesting, what it has to do with you, and our original questions. I promise you that it does, and I will be tying all these loose ends together quite soon.

A Little Fun and Speculation

But just before we move on, let's have a little fun with this idea...

Imagine that you could separate the two entangled particles by several light-years, then apply an action, such as spin, to one which would be *immediately* duplicated in the other. At the risk of making everyone cringe by using a sci-fi term: sub-space radio. Morse code started off with such simple principles, and within a century the technology had raced ahead to radio, TV, radar, and satellite transmissions.

Yes – the bright girl at the back? Yes, well done. Of course you *would* need a 'physical interface' at both ends of the communication. But the California Institute of Technology is already on it. Physicist H. Jeff Kimble and his colleagues have declared that they have achieved the first realisation of entanglement for one "spin excitation" stored jointly between two samples of atoms. 'In the Caltech experiment, the atomic ensembles are located in a pair of apparatuses 2.8 meters apart.' **[40]**

"a pair of apparatuses 2.8 meters apart" ?
I think Marconi and Logie-Baird started with less.

Quantum Information

In our typically human way, we have once again detected a phenomenon, we're attempting to control it, and we're wondering what we can do with it. (We've been doing this for a long time – think 'fire'.)

And one of the greatest needs in this modern society of ours is the manipulation and storage of data, which may be possible at quantum level. The idea is that clouds of atoms could be used as a 'quantum memory' which would exploit quantum phenomena such as entanglement, superposition, and multiple spin-states.

"To me this is a major step forward,"
says Bill Munro, an expert in quantum communications at
Hewlett Packard's research laboratory in Bristol, UK.
...in theory [quantum computers should] be able to
perform billions of calculations simultaneously. [41]

What is less obvious, but to me far more important, is the implicit realisation that quantum level data handling would massively increase the *amount* of data that *could* be handled, since even a single photon can have several different quantum states *simultaneously*, as opposed to the more normal 0/1 state of the electronic binary bit that we currently use.

In other words, if CPUs and memory chips are currently the size of a postage stamp, how would it be if that same data could be handled and stored by something the size of a few molecules?

I feel I should say at this point that a part of me couldn't give 'two hoots' what the physicists are playing with. I've found over the years that anything really worth having will percolate through to the general population - for example mobile phones and laptops - without me having to worry about it. So I magnanimously let them continue playing with their toys while I dig my ditch. But…

Anybody guessed yet where this is leading?

A Summary / Simplification

I mentioned earlier that I *would* explain the reason for discussing quantum phenomena in relation to my original questions.

At this point I feel that I have no choice but to 'go out on a limb' and present what I feel are the key discoveries that quantum research has revealed so far; otherwise this book would be entirely taken up with quotes, references and documentation, and there is simply not enough space here.

If you feel that you cannot take 'on faith' any of the following conclusions, then *do* feel free to initiate your own research, and to reach your own conclusions.

1. Quantum research is incredibly subtle and requires extensive expertise in both physics and mathematics.

2. Only two of the already 'proven' features of quantum interaction, 'entanglement' and 'spin', have been discussed above.

3. At quantum level, discrete particles do not exist – the factors detected are more akin to basic 'forces' such as gravity, attraction, interaction and spin.

4. Quantum level interaction appears to be multi-dimensional – we've long ago left behind the simplicity of the familiar 3 dimensions that existed even at sub-atomic level.

5. At quantum level everything appears to be connected to everything else – the idea of 'separateness' begins to break down.

6. At quantum level 'distances' begin to look at the same time non-existent, and infinite.

7. At quantum level 'time' appears not to exist – as if time, like gravity as Einstein suggested, is merely an 'attribute' of what we consider to be the normal 3 dimensions, not an 'absolute' in its own right.

8. Quantum level storage and calculation of information would be of an inestimable order of magnitude greater than that produced by current technology.

"The universe on a very basic level could be a vast web of particles which remain in contact with one another over distance, and in no time."
- Physicists R. Nadeau and M. Kafatos

Of course you want to know "What has all this got to do with me?"

What could be more to do with you,

than the question of Consciousness?

Chapter 17: Consciousness

"Few people have the imagination for reality."
- Goethe

"Man will occasionally stumble over the truth, but usually manages to pick himself up, walk over or around it, and carry on."
- Winston Churchill

The human brain, in a male, weighs about 3 pounds.

As we've seen, as time went on it became necessary for the various disciplines such as mathematics and physics to work more closely together – their research *had* to become more of a joint effort. Once again, this is what the hairless ape is so good at: teamwork.

Then another interested party entered the discussion: the biologists. My understanding is that the conversation went something like this:

"Hey, guys, *we* also have a problem. We've studied the brain for decades, and where at first we thought that consciousness might be carried out at cellular level, we realised that there simply weren't enough cells. Then we thought that it might be at synaptic level, but there simply aren't enough synapses."

"How do you mean – not enough synapses?"

"Well, whichever way you look at it, there simply is not enough storage in the human brain for what it is able to contain: encyclopaedias of data, decades of detailed memories, even down to individual smells and tastes from one's childhood. And that's just storage! Think of what would be necessary for the moment-to-moment computations: decisions, short-term and long-term planning, the subtlety of emotions, minute judgements... Basically, it's just not possible for the brain, as we understand it, to *do* that! And it's no good just saying 'Ooh, what a wonderful organ it is.' - that explains nothing."

"We see your problem. But what can we do about it?"

"Well, do you know of any other possible way that the brain could store *that* amount of data – to put it simply: orders of magnitude greater than the currently most advanced super-computer?"

"Hmmm... well, it's funny you should mention this, because we were just talking..."

"The quantum mind or quantum consciousness is a protoscientific hypothesis that posits a connection between consciousness, neurobiology, and quantum mechanics. ... The quantum mind hypothesis claims that only quantum mechanics is capable of explaining conscious experience." [42]

The idea that consciousness may be quantum based has been around for a surprisingly long time.

In 1924 Alfred Lotka proposed that the mind controls the brain by modulating quantum jumps.

Herbert Fröhlich, the British physicist, in 1968 suggested that condensation similar to Bose-Einstein can be achieved in nature by biological organisms which are in a non-equilibrium state. (-whatever that is.)

Evan Walker in 1970 proposed a synaptic tunneling model in which electrons can "tunnel" between adjacent neurons. (-we're talking worm-holes, here. I love these guys.)

Nick Herbert, a physicist, has been even more specific on the similarities between Quantum Theory and consciousness. Herbert thinks that consciousness is "a pervasive process in nature" and that it is "as fundamental a component of the universe as elementary particles and forces".

And so on, and so on.

Point to Note

It should be understood that any theories along these lines must, by the normal principles of The Scientific Method, be considered to be conjecture and even pseudo-science. So far, no repeatable experiments have produced results that can be considered a 'scientific proof' of these ideas.

Despite the lack of 'hard' scientific evidence many eminent scientists find this line of reasoning to be
- not just the only possible explanation for the existence of consciousness,
- but also the only possible way that consciousness *could* function.

In other words, because of the very transcendental nature of consciousness – in the sense of it being out of place in the tick-tock universe – it therefore *must* be inexorably linked with, and function because of, an environment which is vastly different from our familiar 3 dimensions.

Point of Interest

It would be good to remind ourselves that these same scientists, these dried and dusty academics, are the same people who originally wanted to present the rest of the tribe with a nice, neat 'box of Lego'.

No-one wanted more than they to finally get to the bottom of these mysteries; to discover the last, smallest basic particle; to sum up any aspect of the universe in a very mechanistic way.

For most of them this *is* why they became scientists, because of the belief that all things could be known, could be discovered, could be defined in simple terms. I'm sure that no-one is more unhappy than they are with their own discoveries.

Yet the overall feeling within their work is that they admit that they *cannot deny* what they are finding; as human beings, rather than as scientists, they feel that there is too much at stake to take a dogmatic, doctrinal view.

Richard A. Mould (Professor Emeritus, Department of Physics and Astronomy, State University of New York), is currently seriously investigating quantum-consciousness to be explored and defined by mathematics. [43]

The work of Dr Huping Hu is also receiving a great deal of attention, especially since his proposed method of data storage is linked to 'quantum spin states' (which we touched on earlier).

"The spin-mediated consciousness theory is a theory that says quantum spin is the seat of consciousness... According to this theory, consciousness is intrinsically connected to the spin process and emerges from the collective

dynamics of spin states and the unity of mind is achieved by quantum entanglement of these mind-pixels." [44] [45]

"We postulate that consciousness is connected to quantum mechanical spin since said spin is embedded in the microscopic structure of spacetime and may be more fundamental than spacetime itself." [46]

Personal Opinion (before we move on)...

It is in the nature of human beings to seize on any new discovery or theory and use it to justify their own opinions or arguments. (Not me, of course.) And so the inevitable has happened with regard to 'quantum-consciousness' which has now simply overtaken the golden ratio in being misunderstood, misquoted, and misappropriated for the personal use of people *outside* of that field.

Where we somehow expect the scientists to use or abuse this field of speculation to their own ends, in fact they are being very cautious – 'won't get fooled again' (see the section of this book on Scientists, and especially phlogiston) – and progressing cautiously and commendably.

In fact it's the 'happy amateurs' who have been jumping out of the woodwork this time, and using this line of research to justify every possible line of mysticism: *"astrology, homeopathy, ghosts, angels, precognition, telepathy, alien abduction, acupuncture, and even how to achieve multiple orgasms".*

My own personal warning bells start when I'm asked to join a club, buy a DVD, or even, heaven help us, 'own the T-shirt'. (You know who you are.)

Because these things are, to me, just the tip of the iceberg of one of the most obnoxious aspects of human nature: certain unscrupulous people will see the opportunity to set themselves up as 'leaders', 'masters', or 'gnostics'.

Even people who we could describe as having 'the best will in the world' can fall prey to their own fantasies of being an advisor, a teacher, an informer.

They say: "Let me show you these things. I have the knowledge."

The hidden inference is, of course, that *you* are a lesser being, who cannot progress or understand without their help.

And this is what I find most obnoxious: the selling of the idea of stratification, in people, in knowledge, in understanding; what my friend Sandra correctly labelled 'the hierarchical approach' in the control of others.

From the beginning of this book I have tried to stress that I feel that it *is* possible to walk your own path, to amass and understand the knowledge around you, and to reach and trust in your own conclusions. This, I believe, is a fundamental, and is absolutely necessary in order to find one's own personal answers, happiness and peace of mind. But of course it also takes practice, great strength, and the ability to throw that crutch away; and the ability to stand up to those 'gurus' and say, "No. Actually you don't know more than I do. We're all just human beings, with the same kind of brain; with the same hopes, fears, dreams and self-delusions. We are *all* learning, and if you suggest that you alone are privy to the truth, then, I'm sorry, but you are mistaken."

*

And so, we have effectively come to the end of my journey.

I hope you have enjoyed walking my path with me.

I've no idea what time it is now. The light is blazing through a crack in the curtains, the birds are singing, the milkman has just delivered, and the fig-rolls are all gone (-I'll regret that tomorrow).

My tea has gone cold; maybe a fresh one? As my mother would say, "When all else fails, put the kettle on."

I sit here now, and I feel very still, very quiet.
It seems strange to think that I was
ever worried about anything.

The sounds of the day wash over me, my mind gently sinks down to... that nameless place inside me that I always knew was there.

At the same time I open my eyes, and reach out with all of my senses into the universe. And feel it humming, vibrating with life and vigour.

My eyes fill with tears.

It's all so beautiful.

Chapter 18: A Telling Off

And the end of all our exploring will be to arrive
where we started and know the place for the first time.
- T. S. Eliot

(This actually happened.)

"What! You can't end it just like that!" cries Hazel.

"Aw, c'mon now Haze. You know how I feel about this," says I.

"No, no, no. You can't do this to them. They're depending on you for an ending, for a conclusion."

"Look – I've said before… I'm more than happy to collate all the information and put it into easy, descriptive terms, but I really do NOT want to make up people's minds for them. If I do *that* then I'll become what I always despised – someone who preaches, who sets themselves up as an authority, who says 'I know best, I've got it sussed, listen to me.'"

"Yes, yes, I understand that," says Hazel, "but this is part of what writing a book is all about."

"But when I've given talks," I whine, "I've been able to just stop at that point, and sort of hold out my hands, raise my eyebrows, and wait for them to…"

"Yes, but that's because they, and you, know that they can then ask questions, query points, ask for more detail – it's totally different, you idiot!"

"But Hazel, this is not like writing a novel: beginning, middle, end… you know – 'the butler dunnit'."

"I agree. But it's even less like giving a talk. They *are* depending on you to round it all up, and fill in the gaps. They *can't* ask questions, so you'll have to take that into account, and provide an ending."

"You mean… tell them what I *really* think?"

"Yes," sighs Hazel, "the conclusions *you've* come to. John, you've asked them to walk the path with you; so that's what they'll really be interested in – what *you* found."

"Well… I suppose there'll be no harm done, so long as they know where I'm coming from?"

"Exactly."

"And if they don't actually like what I say, then they can always just decide that *my* conclusions are a load of crap."

"Exactly."

"Well... the main thing always *was* just to summarise the information. They can use whatever bits of it they like, however they like, to fill in the gaps in their own big pictures, yes?"

"They will anyway. So, come on, give us an ending!"

Sigh. "Well, ok – but I'm always worried that people who go out on a limb like this tend to end up being nailed to a piece of wood."

"Pretentious bastard. You're not that important! Just get on with it. I want to read the ending."

How to do this... how to do this....

How do you show a path of thinking, where all the various steps and gathered ideas have very slowly dovetailed together over a long period of time to form an overall picture.

Remember, I'm not talking about some scientific quest, ever so technical, backed up with formulae and 'proofs'. I'm talking about Mr Average, sat up in bed at 3 in the morning just trying to make some personal sense of what the hell it's all about. And especially, to him, personally. What else matters?

Oh yes, there *have* been moments of revelation, moments of realisation, and definitely moments of letting go of long-held preconceptions.... But we're talking about years of searching, mulling things over, search for more information to fill in the gaps, throw that old information out because it doesn't make sense any more... everything leading, as is always the case of course, to this very moment.

Yeah, got it! I know... let's drag out the contents of the melting-pot, and line-'em up!

So can I finally answer the 'melting pot' questions that I started with?

Yes, I think I can:

LOVE

Why does broken love hurt so much?   Why is love so rewarding?

Because it feels as if there is a
literal physical bond that's been
stretched and even broken.

Because it feels as if there a literal
physical bond that's always been
there, and just gets stronger.

The only answer that makes any sense to me to explain the power and the importance of love in our lives, is that, contrary to the way we've been brought up – thinking of love as an author's subplot, as a poet's daydream – it really is a physical connection between living beings.

Love is a real force, a dimension, a 'connectivity' between us all. Which is why separation causes so much pain…
…and true love feels like it shakes your reality!

Remember "what could those other dimensions be?" Love is one of those 'connectivities'; a real, literal connection between all living beings, which stretches, flexes, weakens, strengthens, and is literally a part of our being; literally a part of what we are, connecting us all.

ANOMALIES (and other fundamental rules)

Pi

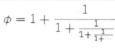

$$\frac{1}{1} - \frac{1}{3} + \frac{1}{5} - \frac{1}{7} + \frac{1}{9} - \cdots = \frac{\pi}{4}$$

$$\frac{2}{\pi} = \frac{\sqrt{2}}{2} \frac{\sqrt{2+\sqrt{2}}}{2} \frac{\sqrt{2+\sqrt{2+\sqrt{2}}}}{2} \cdots$$

- the universe's rule for the creation of both two-dimensional and three-dimensional *circular* shapes.
- fundamental in deciding shape and *motion* within our universe.
- is an irrational number, runs on forever.

The Golden Ratio

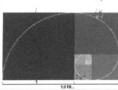

$$\phi = 1 + \cfrac{1}{1 + \cfrac{1}{1 + \cfrac{1}{1+\cdots}}}$$

- has been found in the structure of many objects in nature.

- is an 'irrational' number which seems to 'extend' into infinity.

Fibonacci Series

1, 2, 3, 5, 8, 13, 21, 34, 55, 89, 144, 233, 377...

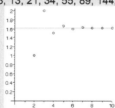

- appears in natural reproductive cycles.
- appears in the musical scale.
- when extended upwards, becomes the golden ratio.
- 'extends' into infinity.

The most fundamental rules of nature and the universe extend into, or 'grow out of', infinity. Again, we have no practical nomenclature for these – to say that a number is 'irrational' does not even come close to expressing its true nature. These three rules, and probably many others as we discover them, appear to 'grow out of infinity' *into* our 3 dimensions.

In fact, the universe doesn't seem to give a damn about my 'fear' of infinity. It doesn't care how people feel about how it works – it just goes ahead and works the way that it does, anyway.

This is about how the universe functions, *whether we exist or not*.

LIFE and GROWTH

In whatever form is most appropriate, life emerges and expands to fill *any* available gap, whether it is spatial, social, or environmental. Here on this planet, life is not the exception; it is the rule.

The growth processes of life may be fractally based.
Fractals are tiny, simple pieces of information, repeated recursively, with incredible potential for expansion and growth.
Fractal information seems to 'extend' into infinity.

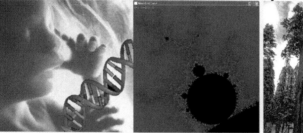

The principles of growth could be (must be?) very simple algorithms, in order to store such complex growth potential in such tiny storage areas.

Even when we set up 'artificial' models which emulate growth, they show a proclivity to extend into, or 'grow out of', infinity.
Life appears to grow so readily out of matter that one would almost think that this is the true purpose of matter; and in fact ultimately it's hard to draw a dividing line between the two.

The amount of energy it must take to 'grow' life, then extend it's capabilities through generation after generation, is inestimable; again another anomaly never even approached by scientists. (I'm not talking about food and drink – that's just tick-over fuel.) That energy must also be one of the 'connectivities' produced down at quantum level, although I prefer to visualise it as a constant 'throughput' or 'flow' from that place out into these 3 dimensions, constantly being passed through one generation to the next.

MATHEMATICS

Mathematics is just a tool, like a ruler. Even so, it is probably the most advanced form of conceptual, comparative thinking that the human race has invented.

It doesn't actually 'do' anything by itself. But it is used by all the other disciplines such as engineering, physics, even biology, to measure and to understand their results.

Mathematics can be used to describe and to examine incredibly complex, and at the same time incredibly subtle, ideas.

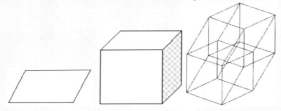

Even the most precise and non-emotional tool that the human race has ever invented has in some marvellous way 'given the game away'.

As it progresses to higher levels, mathematical logic simply must allow for more than 3 dimensions, or if you prefer 'has discovered' greater than 3 dimensions, otherwise the equations do not balance.

The deeper we look, mathematically, into the nature of things, the more all the various previously disparate findings of the different disciplines - chemistry, physics, biology et al - begin to align into a more coherent single concept which encompasses all the ideas and concepts which for so long have been considered 'separate' and unfathomable.

DOWN THE RABBIT HOLE – QUANTUM PHYSICS

At quantum level, discrete particles do not exist - they are more like forces with almost 'zero size'.

Quantum level interaction appears to be multi-dimensional.

At quantum level the idea of 'separateness' begins to break down.

At quantum level 'distances' look non-existent, or infinite.

At quantum level 'time' appears not to exist.

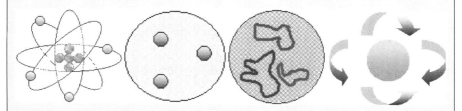

The very fabric of reality (- I've been waiting to use that phrase!) disappears into, or emanates from, a multi-dimensional, timeless infinity.

At the heart of all matter there is a multidimensional, totally connected, timelessness.

CONSCIOUSNESS

"The spin-mediated consciousness theory is a theory that says quantum spin is the seat of consciousness and the linchpin between mind and the brain."

"We postulate that consciousness is connected to quantum mechanical spin since said spin is embedded in the microscopic structure of spacetime and may be more fundamental than spacetime itself."

It would seem that consciousness itself is inexorably connected with, and probably emanates from, quantum level infinity – where reality is multi-dimensional, all particles are connected, and time has no meaning.

Consciousness itself is connected with and emanates from this quantum infinity.

This is probably not just the only possible explanation for the existence of consciousness, but also the only possible way that consciousness *could* function.

So can I finally answer the questions that I started with?

Chapter 19: A New Day

It's 1956, and a 4 year-old boy, in shorts, t-shirt and sandals, throws open the front door and launches himself through the air, out over the three stone steps leading down from the front of the house, and lands clang! on the grating of the metal coal chute. He opens the wooden gate carefully to prevent it from squeaking, then settles himself on the front wall, legs dangling, and leans his head back to feel the new morning sun.

Joyce will come out soon, and Little Peter, and that new bloke Peter Xephonsus (and none of us can say his name properly, and he says his family aren't Catholics, and they aren't Protestants, and the kids say you have to be one or the other, and he says you don't), and maybe Fancy Alan, who talks a lot, and has too much money, and is 'spoiled', which means you don't trust him or else he'll get you into trouble. And we'll play hide and seek, or walking along walls, or skip the cracks, or 'allies' with glass marbles into the depressions in the flags, if someone has enough allies they've not lost down the grid. And we don't play boys' games or girls' games, just games, coz the girls are the same as the boys, except they've got to wear skirts.

The sky is very blue and clear; and the street is a cul-de-sac, which is great coz nobody can afford a car in our street so we can have races up and down and across, and you mustn't go further than the cobbler's, coz that's too near the main road; and that's ok, who wants to, you only need three kids and you can make a game.

The little boy sits and waits. He has no concept of time, or boredom. He has no concept of mortality. He has little understanding of 'past', and absolutely no idea of 'future'; there is only 'now'. He is innocent beyond innocence. But even innocence is a state. This little boy is just being.

*

I knew I could never recapture that feeling. I wished I could, very much. But growing up, growing old, means learning the blunt, hard truth about life, about being alive, and about the inevitability of death. How I envied that little boy his innocence, his innate happiness of... just being. Drugs, religion, choose what you will – these are the things whereby people try to recapture that lost feeling, the past child in themselves that they mourn for.

Of course I did make 'that' deal, didn't I – with myself? The 'truth', whatever it would cost me, however harsh it might turn out to be. So I can never find that little boy inside myself again, can I.

Can I?

*

On the upper floor of the courthouse in the waiting area, the man in the suit stands immobile, hands behind his back, projecting calm, but filled with quiet terror. The accusations that have been made against him are every father's worst nightmare. If it's decided that there's even a grain of truth, then he knows that he will be stigmatised, by all friends, by all family; everything he has worked for, his reputation, his life, will simply be destroyed. And he will never see his lovely daughter again.

Reaching deep inside, he recalls the teachings of the sages, and at least manages to still the shaking in his body and his hands. But the sages are too far away now, and were never real people, just clever words. How would... his father (now dead) deal with a situation like this? Yes, he can see him clearly... with calmness, with quiet dignity, with soft, clear words. With the knowledge that at least he knows the truth – even if no-one else does; he knows – deep inside himself! He held her first! He made that tiny baby a promise, and he kept it!

A commotion from the other waiting area, where the mother and daughter are waiting. Some shouting - uncharacteristic of a courthouse, surely? The social worker walks around the corner shaking her head, and the man prepares himself for the worst. She never did approve of him, or the idea of a father looking after a daughter alone, and then when the daughter chose to live with the mother, she approved. But the social worker gives him an unexpected smile, and leans over so that only he can hear, "Your daughter would like you to take her out on her birthday."

He can hardly speak. "How did you do this?"

"*I* didn't; it's because she loves you", she says with a smile.

Later, he sits in the park opposite the courthouse for a while, looking back at the building. Three floors, and all full of people… not doing for themselves, not spending their lives feathering their own nests, but spending each day making sure other people are protected.

He feels his eyes begin to fill with tears, and knows this to be the start of his return to the human race – his recognition that he is a part of it. And wants to be.

But no time for tears, now. There's still too much to do.

He stands and prepares to go; he grits his teeth, and clenches his stomach...

…for a decade.

*

"Dad, are you sure you're ok?"

We've gone to visit Liz, who's not long out of hospital. This is a joy for me; Liz is well again, and I'm taking my daughter to meet her for the first time. Oh yes, I know, I know - the proud father… but my daughter is now a month past her 21st birthday, and is turning into a beautiful young woman, and is also my best pal. And I love bringing my best pals together; but now it's backfiring because they've both been sitting there cackling and talking about boys, even though there are two and a half decades between them, until I've had to put my hands over my ears and say, "I'm still your father, you know!"

Sonia's concerned because I've sunk into a reverie, and she had to call me a few times. "No," I tell her, "it's ok." But she's concerned, so I explain.

"Actually," I say, "I'm always jealous of people whose changes come gradually, but it's never been that way for me. I don't know why. *My* personal changes always feel like a build up of something… then bang, I'm different – I've moved on. Not the same."

"If you're sure…?"

"I'm fine love, thanks."

So, to the sound of their comforting chatter I sink deep once more. I'm at the end of a disastrous relationship, trying to make sense of what happened.

I let the ideas flip past me like a slideshow. Sorting. Shuffling. Ouch. No, go back. Look at that again. Ok I can do this, I can do this...

And I begin to realise that I can never *really* know her, never really know the reasons... ever.

Flip, sort, shuffle, ouch. Do it again. Face it again. Yes, there's the thought – no denying it, look at it you bastard! Look at it! If she really wanted you she would be here now. Here. Now. But she isn't.

And right at the end of the slideshow, there's just me.

She's made her decision, I know that now. But this is about me, now.

How did I get here?

Because I walked. When it got too painful. I walked.

Why? I could have stayed. I could have subsumed myself in her needs, her reality. But I didn't. Why?

I'm on my feet, pacing. Nearly there, nearly there.

Liz comes back into the room carrying tea, looks at me, puts the cups down.

"Oh, sweetheart...", she says.

"I'm ok. Really."

"Ok to go, Dad?" says Sonia, looking up at me, concerned.

"Ok to go." I say with a smile.

"Stop. Stand still," commands Liz. "Close your eyes."

I trust Liz implicitly.

"Be still, very still," she says.

I think I'm hyperventilating, but I sink down again and try to find that calm place.

"Where are you now?" asks Liz. "Tell me where you are."

"I'm on the edge of a cliff," I say.

"What can you see?"

"Clouds and blueness."

"And what are you going to do?"

The universe is very still. I take a breath, "Fly... I'm ready to fly."

I open my eyes.

"Is that really me? Is that who I really am?"

"Yes, that's who you really are. What did you see before?"

"Whenever I looked inside, all I saw was the crap, the pain, layers on layers of it, years and years of it, and I thought *that* was me. It's hard, but I *can* push it aside like curtains and see it for what it is – layers covering up... and if I look further...", there are now tears running down my cheeks. "Is that really me?" I say quietly.

"That's really you."

Liz, because she's only human, is now looking really smug.

"And you knew. You knew. All the time!" I say pointing my finger.

"Yup!" she laughs. I think her grin could now light a fire.

Liz says quietly, "And her?"

"I know now, she could never join me here. Never stand at my side."

"No. She could never join you there, and make the leap of faith, of life."

"And you knew this all along."

"Yes. But you had to find it out for yourself."

"Dad," says Sonia, holding my hand, "What now?"

"I have absolutely no idea," I say, "- for the first time in my life. Wow!"

The 4 year-old boy leaps the steps, and sits on the wall, feeling the sun on his face, waiting for his friends to come out to play.

And he's always there inside me when I need him, because he always has been. He *is* me. I just forgot for a while.

A new day...

I climb out of my bed, walk over to the window and throw open the curtains. The sunlight of a new day streams in, bathing me in warmth.

My mother, my daughter, my friends, I know you are out there, and the thought that you are alive in the same world fills me with joy.

I open the window and let the sounds of the day wash over me: neighbours talking, a soft cacophony of radio, television, mobile-phones; the muted roar of the traffic, in the distance a train clicking along its tracks, and two, three, no four jets arching gracefully across the sky.

I close my eyes, and in my mind I rise up, higher and higher, to look down on the vast, wonderful kaleidoscope of it all: matter busily transforming into so many hurrying, scurrying creatures, so intent with their plans, rushing, rushing, alive with the joy of it all, whether they realise it or not.

In France an exhausted team of doctors working through the night have finally found the cure for a disease which has eluded them for 18 years.

On the other side of the world, unpublicised and behind closed doors, an accord is signed between two nations which will finally end their age-old history of pointless killing, the reason for which is a forgotten memory.

In sunny Florida three hundred people work as one to prepare the shuttle for its next flight, to take us all one step closer to leaving the Mother, and the next stage of our evolution.

In Sweden, an international symposium is comparing results on the latest tests for a cancer vaccine; while in the next building they're comparing notes from four different countries' experiments on entangled particles, excited about the figures, speechless at the implications for us all…

In Manchester, throughout England, throughout the world, a major percentage of the population have dedicated themselves to making sure that the rest of us are warm, and fed, and free from pain. Did you say the word 'Profit'? Don't be silly - profit never came into it. These people do what they do because it's *who they are*. If it takes all our spare resources to feed, clothe and minister to the sickly, the weak and the old, then SO BE IT. This *is* the definition of civilisation. This *is* what civilisation was always about. This *is* what society is for. Take your silly money games elsewhere.

Sharing, caring, communicating - verbally, artistically, electronically, cybernetically - building a web… slowly building a connected consciousness.

In a four-poster bed in New England an old man dies screaming, too late realising the pointlessness of his life, clawing to hang on to the last few moments. What could have been…

In a bed made mainly of sacking, a forty-year old Indian mother is dying of old age and overwork. Holding the hands of her two eldest children, while the others and their grandchildren stand at the foot of the bed, she sighs contentedly knowing that she has done her best, and knowing that she can now go to her rest. All is as it should be…

In Lytham St Annes, a couple are close to tears, exhausted and clinging to each other after their lovemaking. They are overwhelmed and speechless at what they found together, that what they thought was just sex has now become so much more. As they rest and look into each other's eyes, they feel as if they are melting into each other. They can now talk to each other with their eyes, their hearts, their minds, their bodies…

In New Brighton, a pale skinned red-haired girl of almost fully Irish descent screams as she bring her child into the world. Close by, the father, a mixture of Caribbean and white, feels helpless and frantic that he cannot take this pain away from the woman he loves. And the handsome, beguiling little boy they have made together will change the world. How could it be otherwise…

In Liverpool, a psychotherapist restrains herself from reaching over to hug her client, a woman whose life has been destroyed by watching her sister and family die in front of her eyes, through one man's malice. This woman will never trust a man again. Three years later, the client is standing shyly at the door as the therapist is leaving the hospital. She introduces her new fiancé, then throws herself forward to hug the therapist who gave her back her life.

And underneath it all: the energy of the source, the infinite, streaming out from the centre of every particle, out, into and through every consciousness, connecting every particle, every mind, back to the Oneness from which it all originates.

Out in the corridor someone says, "What I really mean is…", and the other says, "Oh, I didn't realise…" Musical composition is done in the mind, not on paper. In the same way human communication is done mind to mind; the words are just the vehicle.

In a house in Afghanistan, a family sit eating their evening meal when an American soldier kicks in the door. The father rises slowly, looks at the alien creature dressed in fatigues festooned with bullets and small bombs, and stares at the only visible part of the man – his eyes. The father says softly, "What gives you the right?", and after a moment the embarrassed soldier backs out into the street. That evening he speaks to his commanding officer, as have ten other soldiers that day. And the word goes back up the line…

In a garret in Birmingham, a man eating cold baked beans for his evening meal, whose electricity has just run out, has just realised what love really is.

A woman in the next street laughs out loud realising her own folly, and knows how to make it better the next time.

I hear the arguing, the gunshots, the violence, the bullying; all of these are the hopeless, plaintive cries of people who are desperately trying to retain their own redundant sense of separateness.

Too scarred and too scared to reach out, to trust – damaged by those who raised them, or taught them. This chain can and must be broken, and the damaged ones healed.

In Rochdale, a woman closes her eyes and reaches back over 40 years to face her dead father, and finally has the strength to cry out, "How dare you! How could you? I was just a child, you bastard! It was your job to protect me!"

And realising what she has now become, what she has risen above, what she has made of herself by herself and with the help of others, she smiles quietly at the joy and love she sees within herself; then packs her bag and gets ready for the first lesson she will teach. And so the chain is broken.

*

Time to get dressed now, and go out into the world. Open the front door. Hey, milk on the doorstep - how good is that?

"Hi, Ken! How's it going?" A word, just a word; but he knows he's acknowledged and worthwhile. And it cost me... some breath, and a thought.

"Nora! Yes, love, I'm fine, thanks." Nora spends half of every day wearing an oxygen mask, but still insists on popping next door to make sure that *I'm* alright!

"Soyab! My man – gimme five." When I first met Soyab all I saw was the skull-cap, the long skirt, and the beard halfway down his chest. Until he reached over, touched me on the arm, and said, "Awright mate? 'Ow's it goin'?" in a full Bolton accent. I'm doing the America street patois in an attempt to irritate Soyab into teaching me the proper Asian salutation – but the fact is, he's better educated and speaks better English than I do.

I hear the ambulance rushing through the village.

The white lines on the road.

The traffic lights blinking.

The new dentist's, the bank, the accountant's, the solicitor's.

The women's refuge, the hospital, the local college where I can even get courses for free! To learn about...

People helping people.

Sharing, caring, communicating - verbally, artistically, electronically, cybernetically - building a web... slowly building a connected consciousness; slowly realising what we have always been...

Chapter 20: Conclusion – What Am I ?

'We don't even need to try – we are one.'
- Jon Anderson, Tales from Topographic Oceans

I find it hard to remember the old me now. I remember that person – the old me – vaguely, like a fading memory. I'm too busy now, too much to do, don't have the time... to be shy. Don't have the time... not to know you while I can. I'm hungry for your thoughts, your feelings, your experiences. You honour me by sharing them.

There's a world, a universe out there, and I'm part of it. To have been born, to know even a small part of it, to live and *be* part of it, now there's the wonder.

I came into this world, this universe, this existence.

I AM, for a while.

Then I will be gone.

But you see, there's really nothing to be afraid of.
It's no big deal after all.
Because the whole process is the most natural thing there is.
How could it be otherwise?

Let's see what we can do. Let's see what we can build. Let's see what we can achieve. Let's see what we can learn and know. Let's find and fulfil and become what, in essence, we already know we are. Together.

Time, while there is *still* time,
to meet you, to know you,
to love and interact and build with You,

all you other parts of Me.

And underneath and within it all:

the energy of the source, the infinite,
streaming out from the centre of every particle,
out, into and through every consciousness,
connecting every particle, every mind, back
to the Oneness from which all originates
and to which all is connected.

So, what am I ?

I am an extrusion into these three dimensions of a small part of a multi-dimensionality, that I can only think of as 'The Oneness'.

When 'I' die, these three dimensions that I call 'me' will cease and dissolve, and the other dimensions will be reabsorbed back into the Oneness.

As such, my 'personality' will cease – it's only use was to be a part of 'reality';
I would not recognise what I will become as I am reabsorbed back into the source.

The probable point of my existence is for the Oneness to observe and to know itself.

All the people I know and love, including myself, will return to the Oneness, and in fact are already there without realising it.

Afterthoughts

When I think of people, I imagine us as tongues of flame within a fire,
- appearing to be separate,
- connected without knowing it,
- recognising ourselves, and something infinite, in each other.

After one of my talks, Debbie said, "But John, I've always felt this way."

"So have I," I said, shrugging, "for a long time; but now we also have the rationale of science working with us, and we need apologise to no-one for thinking and feeling as we do."

When my father died, he did not end. He just went home. Not to the heaven of the old man with the white beard on the clouds, but to be reabsorbed back into the Oneness from which he came.

My daughter, my family, my beloved friends –

I see you, and know you to be…

part of Me.

Acknowledgements

Sonia Blackledge	"Hey, Dad - good stuff. Why don't you turn it into a book?"
Sandy Bryson	For walking so much of this path with me.
Liz Anderson	For holding up a mirror, and showing me the truth.
Sandra Teale	For her unquenchable enthusiasm.
Hazel Morley	For her boundless encouragement, and righteous criticism.

And a big thank-you to all my family, my friends and acquaintances – Jimmy, Melissa, Andy, all of you – who have taught me so much, and made such a difference in my life, and helped me to arrive where I started and know the place for the first time.

Appendix

[1] The golden ratio shown here to 1,050 decimal places:

```
1.6180339887 4989484820 4586834365 6381177203 0917980576
  2862135448 6227052604 6281890244 9707207204 1893911374
  8475408807 5386891752 1266338622 2353693179 3180060766
  7263544333 8908659593 9582905638 3226613199 2829026788
  0675208766 8925017116 9620703222 1043216269 5486262963
  1361443814 9758701220 3408058879 5445474924 6185695364
  8644492410 4432077134 4947049565 8467885098 7433944221
  2544877066 4780915884 6074998871 2400765217 0575179788
  3416625624 9407589069 7040002812 1042762177 1117778053
  1531714101 1704666599 1466979873 1761356006 7087480710
  1317952368 9427521948 4353056783 0022878569 9782977834
  7845878228 9110976250 0302696156 1700250464 3382437764
  8610283831 2683303724 2926752631 1653392473 1671112115
  8818638513 3162038400 5222165791 2866752946 5490681131
  7159934323 5973494985 0904094762 1322298101 7261070596
  1164562990 9816290555 2085247903 5240602017 2799747175
  3427775927 7862561943 2082750513 1218156285 5122248093
  9471234145 1702237358 0577278616 0086883829 5230459264
  7878017889 9219902707 7690389532 1968198615 1437803149
  9741106926 0886742962 2675756052 3172777520 3536139362
  1076738937 6455606060 5921658946 6759551900 4005559089…
```

[2] The Fibonacci Series within the musical scale.

Note in Scale	A	A	D	F	E	C
Frequency	440	880	293	176	660	264
Fibonacci Ratio	1/1	2/1	2/3	2/5	3/2	3/5
Relationship	Root	Octave	Fourth	Aug5th	Fifth	Minor3rd

Note in Scale	E	C#	F#	C#	D	F
Frequency	165	1100	733	275	1173	704
Fibonacci Ratio	3/8	5/2	5/3	5/8	8/3	8/5
Relationship	Fifth	Third	Sixth	Third	Fourth	Aug5th

[3] The Fibonacci Series division/conversion to the Golden Ratio.

1/1 = 1,   2/1 = 2,   3/2 = 1·5,   5/3 = 1·666,   8/5 = 1·6,
13/8 = 1·625,   21/13 = 1·61538, and on up to 1.618…

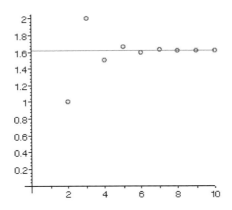

[4] 36 lines of code to create a fractal:

```
Graphics 800,600,16,2
SetBuffer BackBuffer()
maxcolor=255
leftside#=-2 : top#=1.25
xside#=2.5 : yside#=-2.5
xmax=800 : ymax=600
xscale# = xside# / xmax
yscale# = yside# / ymax

For y=1 To ymax
  For x=1 To xmax
    cx# = x # xscale# + leftside#
    cy# = y # yscale# + top#
    zx# = 0
    zy# = 0
    colorcounter = 0
    max = 5 ; 4
    While (zx# # zx# + zy# # zy# < max And colorcounter < maxcolor)
      tempx# = zx# # zx# - zy# # zy# + cx#
      zy# = 2 # zx# # zy# + cy#
      zx# = tempx#
      colorcounter=colorcounter+1
    Wend
    Dot(x,y,colorcounter)
  Next
  Flip
Next

WaitKey
End

Function Dot(x,y,colorcounter)
offset = 0
  r = offset + (colorcounter # 8)
  g = offset + (colorcounter # 4)
  b = offset + (colorcounter # 1)
  Color r,g,b
  Plot x,y
End Function
```

[5] The core 'growth' lines:

```
Graphics 800,600,16,2
SetBuffer BackBuffer()
maxcolor=255
leftside#=-2 : top#=1.25
xside#=2.5 : yside#=-2.5
xmax=800 : ymax=600
xscale# = xside# / xmax
yscale# = yside# / ymax

For y=1 To ymax
  For x=1 To xmax
    cx# = x # xscale# + leftside#
    cy# = y # yscale# + top#
    zx# = 0
    zy# = 0
    colorcounter = 0
    max = 5 ; 4
    While (zx# # zx# + zy# # zy# < max And colorcounter < maxcolor)
      tempx# = zx# # zx# - zy# # zy# + cx#
      zy# = 2 # zx# # zy# + cy#
      zx# = tempx#
      colorcounter=colorcounter+1
    Wend
    Dot(x,y,colorcounter)
  Next
  Flip
Next

WaitKey
End

Function Dot(x,y,colorcounter)
offset = 0
  r = offset + (colorcounter # 8)
  g = offset + (colorcounter # 4)
  b = offset + (colorcounter # 1)
  Color r,g,b
  Plot x,y
End Function
```

Reference List

Many more references can be found on the web for any of the topics mentioned.
For more information on any topic simply search using any of the topic headings shown below, for example "Hyper-Entangled Photon Pairs".

Speed of Light
[1] Zyra
http://www.zyra.org.uk/speed-c.htm
[2] Answers.com
http://www.answers.com/topic/speed-of-light
Faster Than Light
[3] CNN
http://archives.cnn.com/2000/TECH/space/07/20/speed.of.light.ap/[4] ABC
http://spl.haxial.net/universe/light/abc-speedoflight.html
[5] New Scientist
http://www.newscientist.com/article.ns?id=dn2796
The Big Bang
[6] University of Michigan
http://www.umich.edu/~gs265/bigbang.htm
[6] NASA
http://liftoff.msfc.nasa.gov/academy/universe/b_bang.html
Black Holes
[7] Stuart Robbins, Case Western Reserve University, Ohio, majoring in Astronomy and double minoring in Physics and Geology
http://home.case.edu/~sjr16/stars_blackhole.html
[8] NASA
http://imagine.gsfc.nasa.gov/docs/science/know_l2/black_holes.html
[9] New Scientist
http://www.newscientist.com/article.ns?id=dn6151
[10] - Stephen Hawking, A Brief History of Time, Bantam Books
Priestley
[11] Chemical Heritage Foundation
http://www.chemheritage.org/EducationalServices/chemach/fore/jp.html
Einstein
[12] Beto Hoisel
http://www.newciv.org/nl/newslog.php/_v399/__show_article/_a000399-000003.htm
[13] USC Student Computing Facility
http://www-scf.usc.edu/~kallos/gravity.htm
[14] Journal of Young Investigators. 2005. Volume 13.
http://www.jyi.org/news/nb.php?id=623
Hawking
[15] Space.com
http://space.com/news/hawking_bet_040716.html
[16] New Scientist
http://www.newscientist.com/article.ns?id=dn6151
Hubble
http://www.time.com/time/magazine/article/0,9171,757145,00.html
Vatican

http://www.faculty.fairfield.edu/jmac/sj/scientists/secchi.htm
Scientific Method
[17] Science Service
http://www.sciserv.org/isef/primer/scientific_method.asp
Carl Sagan
[18] CarlSagan.com
http://www.carlsagan.com http://en.wikipedia.org/wiki/Carl_Sagan
Pi
[19] Wikipedia
http://en.wikipedia.org/wiki/Pi
[20] Berkeley Lab Computing Services
http://crd.lbl.gov/~dhbailey/dhbpapers/pi-quest.pdf
Golden Ratio
[21] Wikipedia
http://en.wikipedia.org/wiki/Golden_ratio
Fibonacci Series
[22] Wikipedia
http://en.wikipedia.org/wiki/Fibonacci
[23] School of Electronics and Physical Sciences, University of Surrey
http://www.mcs.surrey.ac.uk/Personal/R.Knott/Fibonacci/
[24] GoldenNumber.net
http://goldennumber.net/music.htm
Fractals
[25] Wikipedia
http://en.wikipedia.org/wiki/Fractal
Fractal Growth
[26] European Research Consortium for Informatics and Mathematics
http://www.ercim.org/publication/Ercim_News/enw29/vicsek.html
[27] Journal of National Cancer Institute
http://jncicancerspectrum.oxfordjournals.org/cgi/content/full/jnci;95/10/704
[28] American Association for the Advancement of Science
http://www.sciencemag.org/cgi/content/abstract/284/5420/1677
Crystals
[29] Centre for Computational Materials Science
http://cst-www.nrl.navy.mil/lattice/
Flatland
[30] Alcyone Systems
http://www.alcyone.com/max/lit/flatland/
Hypercube
[31] Wolfram Research
http://mathworld.wolfram.com/Hypercube.html
Supergravity
[32] Scientific American
http://www.sciam.com/askexpert_question.cfm?articleID=000D8EEB-
3D04-13D9-BD0483414B7F0000&ref=sciam&chanID=sa005
Multi-Dimensions
[32] Scientific American
http://www.sciam.com/askexpert_question.cfm?articleID=000D8EEB-
3D04-13D9-BD0483414B7F0000&ref=sciam&chanID=sa005
Atomic Structure
[33] HowStuffWorks
http://science.howstuffworks.com/atom.htm

String Theory / Multi-Dimensions
[34] Wikipedia
http://en.wikipedia.org/wiki/Why_10_dimensions
[35] New Scientist
http://www.newscientist.com/channel/fundamentals/quantum-world
Hyper-Entangled Photon Pairs
[36] American Institute of Physics
http://www.aip.org/pnu/2005/split/754-1.html
[37] Quantum Entanglement
http://www.joot.com/dave/writings/articles/entanglement/quantum-entanglement.shtml
[38] American Scientist
http://www.americanscientist.org/template/BookReviewTypeDetail/assetid/18847;jsessionid=baafs81-MJvJ3p
[39] NASA
http://www.grc.nasa.gov/WWW/combustion/people/vnguyen/Qe/Qe.htm
[40] PhysOrg.com
http://pda.physorg.com/lofi-news-quantum-atoms-entanglement_8891.html
Quantum-based Computer Data
[41] NewScientist
http://www.newscientist.com/article.ns?id=dn8432
Quantum Consciousness / Spin-Mediated Consciousness Theory
[42] Wikipedia definition
http://en.wikipedia.org/wiki/Quantum_mind
[43] Richard A. Mould, Professor Emeritus, Department of Physics and Astronomy, State University of New York
http://ms.cc.sunysb.edu/~rmould/
[44] Wikipedia
http://en.wikipedia.org/wiki/Spin-Mediated_Consciousness_Theory
[45] Huping Hu B.S. M.S. Ph.D. Progress in Physics, 2006, v.3, 20-26
http://www.neuroquantology.com/journal/index.php/nq/issue/view/21
http://www.arxiv.org/abs/quant-ph/0208068v1

Books
Heisenberg, Werner.
Physics and Philosophy: The Revolution in Modern Science.
Harper and Row, 1958.

Heisenberg, Werner.
Physics and Beyond: Encounters and Conversations.
Harper and Row, 1971.

Feynman, Richard. QED:
The Strange Theory of Light and Matter.
Princeton University Press, 1985.

Roger Penrose,
The Emperor's New Mind: Concerning Minds and the Laws of Physics.
Oxford University Press, 1989.

Roger Penrose,
Shadows of the Mind: A Search for the Missing Science of Consciousness.

Oxford University Press, 1994.

Hawking, Stephen.
A Brief History of Time.
Bantam, 1998.

Greene, Brian.
The Elegant Universe: Superstrings, Hidden Dimensions, and the Quest for the Ultimate Theory.
Vintage, 2000.

Internet
Heisenberg and Uncertainty: A Web Exhibit American Institute of Physics
www.aip.org/history/heisenberg/
Measurement in Quantum Mechanics: Frequently Asked Questions edited by Paul Budnik
www.mtnmath.com/faq/meas-qm.html
Discussions with Einstein on Epistemological Problems in Atomic Physics, Niels Bohr (1949)
www.marxists.org/reference/subject/philosophy/works/dk/bohr.htm
The History of Quantum Theory, Werner Heisenberg (1958)
www.marxists.org/reference/subject/philosophy/works/ge/heisenb2.htm
The Copenhagen Interpretation of Quantum Theory, Werner Heisenberg (1958)
www.marxists.org/reference/subject/philosophy/works/ge/heisenb3.htm

Wikipedia
http://en.wikipedia.org/wiki/Quantum_mechanics
http://plato.stanford.edu/entries/qt-quantlog/
http://scienceworld.wolfram.com/physics/topics/EarlyQuantumMechanics.html

Loop Quantum Cosmology Martin Bojowald, Max Planck Institute for Gravitational Physics,
http://relativity.livingreviews.org/Articles/lrr-2005-11/title.html

About the Author

John Blackledge has

- worked for I.C.I. as a test-tube washer

- worked for Costain Engineering as a filing clerk and general purpose fall-guy

- worked for British Nuclear Fuels as a programmer

- worked for Vektor Multimedia as a head of three departments

- has written computer software for over 25 years, and has run his own company creating websites and 3D visualisation software

- has worked as a complaints investigator for the Department of Works and Pensions (child support)

> He will never be accused of literature,
> but doesn't care so long as they
> don't nail him to a piece of wood.

Printed in Poland
by Amazon Fulfillment
Poland Sp. z o.o., Wrocław